D0852730

The TEN GIFTS

Happy —
Healthy —
Free ☆

Enjoy your
Ten gifts —
Robin L.
Silverman

Other Works by Robin L. Silverman

A Bosnian Family
Relaxation for Busy People (audiotape)
Love from Home (audiotape)

The TEN GIFTS

ROBIN L. SILVERMAN

St. Martin's Press 🐏 New York

Book design by Clair Moritz

ISBN 0-312-25229-3

First Edition: May 2000

10 9 8 7 6 5 4 3 2 1

To my family

I LOVE YOU WITH ALL MY HEART

. . . .

Acknowledgments

PEOPLE OFTEN SAY that writing is a lonely business. I know now that is not so. Many, many others have helped create this book, and it has been my absolute pleasure and delight to have them join me in the task.

First, there is God, from whom life and our gifts flow. During the flood and its aftermath, I was continually awed by the beauty I saw emerging around me in spite of the destruction that had taken place. I knew then and now that none of us is ever alone, and that no matter what our dreams, God and the life our Source has created will support them.

On a more earthly note, in the beginning, literally and figuratively, were my parents, Marion and Mel Landew. They showed me how to love life and think of everyone as a potential friend. Thanks to them, I have never been afraid to approach a stranger with a handshake and a smile, a skill that has served me well in gathering these and so many other stories. Their many positive comments about my columns and articles over the years gave me the fuel to keep writing, and their gifts, including my electric typewriter and introductions to their friends in the book industry, made it easier for me to succeed. Their enthusiasm and excitement over the publication of this book is matched only by my own.

My family was equally involved in the creative process, including my husband, Steve, and daughters, Amanda and Erica. When I sometimes wondered why I was doing this, one of them would come into my office with a kiss, a hug or a shoulder rub and I could see love in the effort once more.

I was also energized by two friends who felt like family: Jan Kurtyka and Duane Cariveau. For seven years, my assistant Jan and I shared an office and a small table that served as our mutual desk. She read every word I wrote, showed up at every seminar I gave, and listened to thousands of hours of dreaming and screaming as I marched forward in this quest. Duane, a longtime friend in the marketing and consulting business, consumed thousands of cups of coffee with me and listened avidly as I talked about my stories, manuscripts, and audiences. I could never have made it to the point of publication without him saying, "Way to go, Rob!" every step of the way. I was also blessed by my writer's group, especially friend and author Jane Kurtz, who continually encouraged and inspired me with her own string of successes.

This book could not have been made without the people whose stories are here. They gave me countless hours of interview time, shared feelings and information that people don't often talk about, and trusted me to tell their stories to you. They made it easy for me to write this book, and inspired me to use my own gifts.

There never would have been any book at all if my friend and mentor Azriela Jaffe hadn't coached me in my creation of a proposal that could stand up to the scrutiny of a major publishing house. She helped me clarify what I wanted to say and was an honest, demanding, and compassionate teacher who made sure I said it right.

Then came my wonderful agent, Gareth Esersky, whose energy for this book was unbounded. She brought me a stream of great ideas from editors and kept up my spirits as

I reworked the manuscript again and again before it was accepted. She knows people and knows books, and she also knows how to be a terrific friend.

Gareth led me to Jennifer Enderlin, my editor at St. Martin's Press. I like to tell Jen she's the greatest editor on the planet, because she is. Not only does she have a great eye for content and style; she also knows what makes a book successful. She was willing to go the distance on every part of the project, and as she worked, I learned what true commitment looks, sounds, and acts like. Jen was a gentle and patient guide who helped me understand the intricacies of the book business, and a radiant light for what this book could be for readers. Best of all, she has a terrific laugh, and leaves fabulous voice-mail messages when things go right.

Thanks to Jen, I was able to contact the authors whose endorsements you see on the cover of this book. These people, too, are part of me now, and I feel blessed by their generosity, kindness and support for a stranger.

Then there is the team at St. Martin's Press, many of whom I have never met. The sales force, marketers, publicity people, and designers have all contributed to the process of getting this book from me to you. You would not be holding it now if they had not done their jobs well.

Next, there are you, my dear readers. For ultimately, the purpose of creating this book was so that you could share in its stories and ideas, and most important, its intention, which is that something here will contribute to your personal peace.

To all who played a part in bringing *The Ten Gifts* to life, Thank you. In my finest dreams, I could never have imagined a more loving, generous, or creative group of souls. May your beautiful spirits be blessed a thousand times over for all you have given to me.

From my heart to yours,
Robin Silverman

Nothing can bring you peace but yourself.

—RALPH WALDO EMERSON

Contents

Introduction   xv
1. Discovery.   1
   Peace Progress Step 1: Defining Peace   16
2. The Gift of Faith   20
   Peace Progess Step 2: Using Faith   36
3. The Gift of Love.   40
   Peace Progress Step 3: Through the Eyes of Love   54
4. The Gift of Dreams   57
   Peace Progress Step 4: Creating Dreams   65
5. The Gift of Courage.   72
   Peace Progress Step 5: Just One Thing   84
6. The Gift of Unity   87
   Peace Progress Step 6: Many Hands, One Heart.   97
7. The Gift of Joy 100
   Peace Progress Step 7: Journaling Joy. 114
8. The Gift of Trust 120
   Peace Progress Step 8: A Minute of Trust. 134
9. The Gift of Character 140
   Peace Progress Step 9: Haul Out the Mental Trash . . . 154
10. The Gift of Thanks 158
    Peace Progress Step 10: Bless You!. 172
11. The Gift of Intention. 180
    Peace Progress Step 11: "I Feel Good!" 193
12. Epilogue: A New Life 197
    Peace Progress Step 12: A Prayer for Peace 209
    For Further Information 211

Introduction

IF YOU'VE PICKED up this book, chances are good you've had enough: worry, fear, misery, restlessness, or defensiveness. It really doesn't matter how you came by your discontent; what does matter is that you know you're ready for some peace. This is a good place to start finding it.

I am a lot like you, and like you, I found myself at a point in my life where I was anything but peaceful. Born in the heart of the baby boom, I grew up wanting to have it all, and indeed, I got a lot of it. By the time I was thirty, I had a husband, two daughters, and co-ownership responsibility in three retail stores. In addition, I owned a beautiful but cranky old house filled with way too much stuff. I organized my vacations and correspondence around an extended family spread out over 1,400 miles and chose to be obligated to my synagogue family for more than a decade as a volunteer religious schoolteacher and later as president of the board of directors. I also had 39,000 readers waiting to see fresh material from me in my newspaper column in the *Grand Forks Herald* every Sunday and thousands more seeking new perspectives in my workshops. As the decade wore on, things only became more complicated as my children developed their own skills and interests and I took on more responsibility in our community.

By the time I was forty, I was anything but peaceful. I would rush from one activity to the next, always telling myself, "If I just get this next thing done, *then* I'll feel peaceful." But in the meantime, my mind was saturated with thoughts of what I hadn't finished, didn't fully appreciate, or couldn't do. The fear of whom I might disappoint—including myself—turned into simmering anger, fitful sleep, and an irritable bowel. I kept remembering the biblical saying "Ask and ye shall receive," and the Arab postscript: "and pay for it."

Things went along this way until April 18, 1997, when, in the course of a few hours, I lost every role, possession, and situation I'd used over a twenty-year period to define myself. The Red River of the North, which normally meanders lazily between Grand Forks, North Dakota, and East Grand Forks, Minnesota, billowed into a toxic ocean filled with dead animal carcasses, petrochemical residues from cars and heating oil tanks, river debris, and sewage. Normally fifty feet in width, it grew to almost fifteen miles wide from the meltdown of a brutal winter that dumped more than a hundred inches of snow on the prairie. Although the National Weather Service warned that flooding would be "severe," no one had any idea that the predicted crest would be topped by more than five feet. The Red spills its banks at twenty-eight feet; in 1997 it crested at more than fifty-four.

The disaster wiped out life as I knew it. Overnight, the river claimed our house, my job, and my volunteer work. Suddenly my roles and the expectations that went with them—for better or worse—were moot. The flood also forced my husband, Steve, and me to send our children and his elderly parents away for an indefinite period because we couldn't care for them properly while we were trying to reestablish ourselves. My worst fear, that somehow everything that mattered could be taken from me, had come true.

It was the most liberating moment of my life.

At first, the knowledge that we were all safe and sound was enough. Survival alone was exhilarating. We had escaped, physically unharmed. Moreover, for the first time of my adult life, I had nothing and no one expecting or demanding my care. We had no idea when—make that if—we could go home, so for the foreseeable future, I had no place to go, nowhere I had to be. I also had no deadlines, schedules, or promises to fulfill. With the burden of my complicated life temporarily lifted, I found that I was adrift but surprisingly calm for the moment.

However, this initial pause was quickly challenged by the mountain of responsibilities we faced. Somehow, Steve and I would have to secure a new place to live while our old one was either repaired or demolished. We had bills to pay, so a reliable income was necessary. My congregation was receiving hundreds of offers of assistance from individuals and groups around the country, which kept my phone, fax, and e-mail going day and night. In addition, the government entered our life in a big way, as the Federal Emergency Management Association (FEMA), the Small Business Association (SBA), and National Flood Insurance representatives piled on paperwork and regulations that were the only way we could eventually reopen our flagship store in Grand Forks, the source of most of our personal income.

As I faced the daunting task of rebuilding my life, I knew I'd never be able to do it without the peace I knew I lacked. It was no longer something I wanted just for myself; I sought it also for the people around me who were terrified of what the future might bring. It was not just one friend or two who felt this way: 60,000 of us were in this together, as the flood was the single largest natural disaster in modern American history. (Note: The floods following Hurricane Floyd in North Carolina ultimately affected more people, but no one town suffered as much damage as Grand Forks.)

Our Fargo store quickly became the gathering place for many of the Grand Forks evacuees, and when Steve returned to our temporary apartment each night, he would share stories about many of the people we knew. It soon became obvious that some were thriving while others were fading fast. Although I tried to be compassionate about those who were struggling, instinct told me to pay closer attention to those who were sailing through the recovery process with their humor, love, and kindness intact. In those people, I knew, lay the answer to my question: "How do I find peace?"

Before the flood, I told hundreds of stories in my column and other writings and speeches about finding the good in yourself and others. I'd seen others make their own miracles by reaching deep inside themselves to produce unshakable faith, astounding courage, and unrestrained joy. I'd spent more than a decade reading everything I could find on what sets our spirits and the energy that is their source free. So I began searching, both through the ideas and stories I remembered and the ones I saw unfolding before me daily, for what would help us all establish a firm foundation of personal peace. In time I found it: The Ten Gifts.

What you hold in your hands are the lights that lit a path for me to certainty and wholeness. The gifts are spiritual verbs that come "with the package," so to speak, of human life, treasures from our Creator that provide the sturdy foundation we need to become or create whatever we want. They are proof that we are far more divine and have greater worth to ourselves and other people than we may have thought.

Although you have undoubtedly encountered the gifts before, you may never have heard them defined in these ways or seen what happens when you use them proactively, to improve your life, rather than reactively, just to save it. You have already received these gifts, which can be proved by the fact that you will reach inside yourself and use them when all else fails. Although you don't have to wait for disaster to strike, one thing about being human is that until circumstances get as bad as they can get, most of us don't realize how amazingly good we are. One of the purposes of this book is to give you the pleasure—the delight—of using your gifts not because you have to but because you *choose* to. You're about to see that when you do, you'll never be afraid of life again. And that will give you what you came here to get: personal peace.

For optimum results, I recommend you think of this book not simply as a good read, but as a reliable friend. Take it one chapter at a time and get to know each of your gifts well before moving on. Try the exercise at the end of each chapter several times, on different days, under different conditions. There's no hurry: You have your whole life to enjoy using your gifts. If you take your time and get to know each one well, you'll find your peace just as quickly as someone who digests the whole book rapidly. Either way, you'll discover how richly you are blessed and have the peace of knowing and using your gifts to set yourself free.

But if you're the kind of person who just can't wait to see what happens in the end, try this. Sit up straight in a comfortable chair with both feet flat on the floor and the book on your lap. Close your eyes and take three or four deep breaths through your nose, lifting up from your abdomen and bringing the oxygen up behind your eyes before you release it through your mouth. When you feel relaxed, ask out loud: "What gift best serves me now?" Then open the book at random. Trust that your inner self knows the gift you're ready to use and is showing you exactly what you need to practice at the moment. You also can read the book backward, starting with the gift of Intention and moving forward to Faith. No matter how you explore them, the gifts will serve you well.

I always recommend keeping a journal. But if you hate pen and paper, you can keep an oral history quite nicely by sharing your experiences with your gifts with a close friend or by recording your impressions on an audiocassette. (For a variety of fun ideas on how to keep a journal, see Chapter 7, "The gift of Joy.")

You'll soon see that the gifts were not given to us to use only in times of lack. As things get better for you, I hope you will vow to use your gifts in your happy, healthy life to keep and improve your peace. I believe with all my heart that God gave them to us so we could thrive day in and day out, year in and year out, for the time our spirits live on Earth. If you use and expand your gifts, you will be of far better service to yourself and the world than if you don't. If you've ever spent time with a calm, relaxed person and then found yourself near one who is stressed out and unhappy, you know that the better you feel, the better you make others feel. And that makes the world a little more peaceful for all of us.

Using your ten gifts doesn't guarantee that your life will be disaster-proof in the future, but doing so will add the confidence, control, and satisfaction to get you through trouble with shining colors. These are earthly gifts, not heavenly suggestions or vague promises of a brighter day. They will help you to be response-able, which will make you less afraid of life. And that will likely help you to feel more peaceful and a lot happier.

Besides the gifts, I've shared with you some of the prayers, ideas, and actions I used in those turbulent days and nights to bring a temporary halt to whatever panic or restlessness I was feeling. I hope you find these inspiring and will use them as springboards to create some of your own. They are especially useful when your current situation is so difficult that consciously applying your gifts is impossible.

Like my fellow evacuees, I lost many things in the flood. Not just the sofas, baby crib, and mementos I was collecting in the basement, or the decades of memories and the tens of thousands of dollars we invested to repair our house, which we recently sold to the city because it is slated to be moved to make way for a new, permanent dike. Like many others, I also lost my fear of the future; my doubts that all things eventually come to good; my apathy, arrogance, and anger. I lost them not because I planned or wanted to but because it was impossible not to as I put my gifts to good use. As I continue to do so, I enjoy a lot more love and a lot less fear in my life. And that feels good. Peaceful.

There is nothing in my experience that cannot be duplicated in yours. Indeed, as you read each chapter, you'll see real-life examples of many others who have found their gifts and the subsequent pleasure and peace of using them. As I said earlier, I hope you are inspired to choose to use your gifts now rather than wait until life hands you a circumstance like mine where you must. There is great pleasure in knowing you have these resources at your command and great comfort in their expression.

I'd love to hear about your experiences with the gifts and will do my best to respond if you write to me. Send your letters or questions to me at P.O. Box 13135, Grand Forks, ND 58208-3135. You also can visit me on my Web site, www.robinsilverman.com, where you'll find information about my workshops, tapes, other books, and more.

I wish you peace and the freedom for all of us that it brings.

—Robin Silverman

······································

The TEN GIFTS

CHAPTER ONE

. . . .

Discovery

MY RIGHT HAND moved instinctively to the center console of my Mazda, reaching for the coffee cup that wasn't there. I needed something hot and full of acid to burn a hole through this bad dream and wake me up.

"Boy, what I wouldn't give for a cup of really strong coffee right now," I said through gritted teeth.

Erica, my fourteen-year-old, stared vacantly out the window at the black, lifeless fields. "Everything's closed, Mom. The flood. Remember?"

I nodded. *I wish I could forget!* We were headed south on County Road 18, refugees from the worst flood in modern American history. The Red River of the North had claimed our town, Grand Forks, North Dakota, and its sister city, East Grand Forks, Minnesota, just two days before. We escaped with our lives, our cars, a few items of clothing, and the family photo albums, which was more than most people from what we gleaned from the television and newspaper reports. I had also grabbed two boxes of Passover matzoh from my kitchen counter as I ran out the door, ironically thinking I would be celebrating the Exodus, not living it.

Despite community sandbagging efforts that went on

1

twenty-four hours a day for weeks on end, the river won, cresting a full five feet above predicted levels. Now more than 60,000 of us were off to strange and distant places for the foreseeable future, since the mayors of both cities said it would be weeks before we could even return home to survey the damage.

The two-lane road was pockmarked with scars from the brutal winter that had caused this tragedy. More than 110 inches of snow had fallen on our region in eight blizzards that had already caused enough suffering for a lifetime. We were still recovering from Blizzard Hannah, whose ice and winds knocked out power up and down the Red River Valley for the first few weeks of April, when the flood hit with full force. We had been struggling to stay ahead of Mother Nature for almost a month, and now she not only caught up with us, she forced us out.

I could barely see my husband's teal-green Jimmy up ahead, which was leading our five-car caravan. My Mazda, heavily burdened by the merchandise and materials we managed to scavenge from our family's menswear store, scraped the crumbling asphalt with each bump and bounce. Thankfully, our retail store was dry when we last saw it, although we knew our downtown warehouse probably was destroyed. We filled my car, Steve's, and that of our seventeen-year-old daughter, Amanda, both inside and out, tying box after box of merchandise onto the roofs and shoving merchandise, tape measures, pins, and financial records into trunks, cargo areas, and spaces between and under the seats.

Amanda was plugging along behind Steve in her aging red Tempo. The other minivan and car in our little parade, also packed with goods from the store, belonged to the Haugen family, who had given us refuge over the weekend when the dikes were topped and the lift stations, which kept the city's water flowing normally through the sewer system, failed. We'd left our collie, Lady, on their farm twenty miles west of town as we moved what we could to Fargo, where we had a small, as-yet unprofitable satellite store. We had reservations at the Holiday Inn Express for just five nights, all we could get. After that, we were on our own, since every hotel, motel, bed-and-breakfast, and truck stop was filled to overflowing with evacuees and incoming rescue workers.

I looked in my rearview mirror and could see a line of cars stretching all the way back to the Forks. Ahead of me the picture was the same. Dust- and mud-covered vehicles snaked their way south, filled with grim-faced drivers and passengers. Some were carrying household goods, but most were not. Although the mayor had given those of us living in low-lying areas three days' warning of a possible evacuation, most townspeople thought they were safe from the river, as their homes were well out of the hundred-year flood plain. When the water came bubbling up out of sewers and began pouring down the streets, most escaped with only the clothes on their backs. The road heading north was eerily empty, almost as if what was once there had ceased to exist.

In spite of my lack of caffeine, my hands shook. I gripped the steering wheel so tightly that my knuckles turned white. *What will happen to all of us? How are we going to live?*

It wasn't just the raging waters we were fleeing. A monstrous fire was engulfing the downtown area of Grand Forks. As we watched it on television from the home of friends, it seemed almost surreal. One of our business districts was burning up, even though it was filled with water. No one knew how the fire had started; the media's best guess was that something electrical had shorted out before power was cut to the city.

The fire had already devoured one city block, and its sparks were quickly igniting buildings up to two blocks away. The town's major newspaper, the *Grand Forks Herald*, had already burned to the ground, and our bank was on fire as we left town. Our house was less than five blocks from the fire's last location. The firefighters had no way of battling it, as there was no water pressure from the hydrants due to the failure of the lift stations. They tried dumping chemicals from the air, which didn't work. Last we saw, they were attempting to airlift the floodwater itself and release it on the fire, their only hope of getting the blaze under control.

It felt as if our whole world were coming to an end. *Don't look back*, I said to Steve that morning as we hit the highway. But even though my car was facing south, I couldn't help but look in the rearview mirror every few seconds. Anxiety strangled my desire to make simple conversation with my daughter; fear clouded my vision of what might lie ahead. *I just want to go home. . . .*

Our Fargo store couldn't support our family; it was barely paying its bills. And with our Grand Forks store closed for the foreseeable future, our main source of income was cut off. The winter had already knocked the wind out of our profits, as we were closed or business had been minimal for almost three months. Now it would be weeks, maybe months more before the main store would be open again. I tried to remember how much we had left in our checking and money market accounts. I started to sweat, in spite of the fact that there was still snow on the fields.

"What's wrong, Mom?" Erica asked.

I didn't want to scare her with my fears. I couldn't bring myself to tell my baby that not only were we now homeless, but her father and I were basically jobless as well. Even though I was a writer and public speaker, my income from those activities had come to a halt as the river rose. I hadn't written a word in weeks, and all my regional speaking engagements had been canceled as sandbagging efforts escalated.

"Nothing, sweetheart," I said. "I was just thinking."

Her enormous brown eyes looked sad. "About what?"

My best and only defense was to answer her question with another question. "What are *you* thinking about?"

"My friends. I wonder where they are right now."

"Probably doing the same thing we're doing—trying to find a place to live."

She bit her lower lip.

"Hey," I said as cheerfully as I could, "I'll bet Emily and her family went to their lake cabin. You can try calling when we get to Fargo, okay?"

She nodded.

"And this isn't so bad—we've already had two days of home-cooked meals, and now we'll be eating in restaurants in Fargo. No more Salvation Army truck food," I offered.

"I *like* Salvation Army truck food," Erica replied. "I don't care that you can't tell what it is; it tastes good. Besides, I haven't had to do dishes in a while."

I tried to laugh. "Yep, I guess that's true. I'm kind of fond of their hamburger hotdish myself."

For the weeks we worked to shore up and patrol the dikes, the Salvation Army and Red Cross had provided all our meals and snacks. You could always count on their trucks to pull up just when your longing for a sandwich or a cup of coffee was greatest. I looked in the rearview mirror now, just to see if there might be one behind us. Even watery coffee was better than none. No luck.

"What are we going to do when we get to Fargo, Mom?"

Finally: a question I could answer. "Unpack the cars and get something to eat. Dad is going over to the store to try to get the Grand Forks computers up and running. I'll take you girls to the hotel so you can rest."

Initially, on our escape, we were euphoric that we survived the disaster. We were grateful to be safe, happy to be with friends, and relieved to be in a peaceful place where the air was not cut every few minutes with the sound of emergency sirens or the relentless buzz of patrolling helicopters. We were physically and emotionally exhausted but upbeat, feeling lucky.

But now reality was starting to set in. *There will be no*

rest for you, dear. You'd better start making some calls, fast.
I could feel my heart pounding in my chest. *You're making yourself sick with worry. Stop it!* As one who taught the creative power of thoughts and emotions in my workshops, I knew I wasn't doing myself any good. So I tried some positive thinking: *You've been working night and day for weeks, and now you'll get a much-needed vacation! You won't have to go grocery shopping for a few days, and all the cleaning will be done for you. There will be lots of Grand Forks people down in Fargo—you could have a great reunion at the store!*

But the more I tried to find the silver lining, the worse I felt. As my brain tried to conjure up pretty pictures, my gut instincts were screaming *Liar! Fool! You're a mess, and you know it! This is the worst trouble you've ever been in, so get ready to suffer, babe! No place to live, no job, no money—it's your worst nightmare come true!* The fact was, I didn't need a vacation. I had been barely working for weeks. What I wanted was to go back to my work. I would have loved a reason to buy fresh groceries, as I was sick of eating high-fat, high-salt processed stuff. And what kind of reunion would it be with people who were as upset and disoriented as we?

I knew I didn't want to feel the way I did, so I tried a different approach to shake my fear: distracting myself, looking around for things in my immediate environment that brought me pleasure or peace. Usually just being with Erica could do that, as she is one of the most calm and contented people I know. But today even she was holding back a combination of fearful tears and rage. School had been canceled for the rest of the year, which meant that she and her sister had lost six weeks of coursework. On top of that, there was little chance they would see most of their friends for weeks, and such reunions would occur only if they managed to both escape and return safely.

Looking around, I just got gloomier. The fields, which burst with the promise of new life every summer as the crops hit their peak, were nothing more than hard lumps of black mud at the moment. The trees were bare of both snow and leaves, and looked dead. Alongside the road, there were still some toppled power lines remaining from Blizzard Hannah. The sight of the downed lines deepened the sense of isolation I was beginning to feel. I cracked my window for some fresh air, but only the frigid wind spoke; it was too early for the snow geese to return.

The sight of all this emptiness reflected my feelings that my world, indeed, had come to an end. The 115-year-old home we had painstakingly restored for almost eighteen years was unreachable for the foreseeable future, or might be gone altogether, swept off its aging foundation by the rage of the turbulent water. My marketing job with our store was suspended, not only because our Grand Forks customers were gone but because it was obvious that we would need a separate source of income, and I would have to provide it while Steve tended to the family business. The synagogue over whose board of directors I presided was in one of the worst-hit neighborhoods. Our children would have to be sent to my parents until we could reestablish ourselves. Overnight, everything I owned and all the roles I played were gone. Beneath my worry, strangely, there was something appealing about that. I had nothing to do and nowhere to go but to be where I was, doing what I was doing at the moment.

I craved life, music, joy—anything to shake off the gloom I was fighting. I instinctively reached for my CD player. Whitney Houston's "The Preacher's Wife" burst forth from six speakers. I started to hum, and as I did, I could feel a warm buzz of energy return to my brain. I started to make a mental list of all the tasks I'd have to do to help Steve, take care of the kids, find writing work and more, but it soon became far more than I could remember. As restlessness crept back in, I knew I was going to need more than simple faith to face what lay ahead. What I desperately wanted was what some call "the peace of God," that absolutely sure, comforting certainty that this, too, would pass and all would be well again. Without that peace, I doubted I would have the emotional, spiritual or even physical stamina to rebuild or replace my home, help restore the synagogue and double my income.

THE SEARCH FOR PEACE

How do I find peace, God? I took that question to bed with me that night, and slept more soundly than I expected to. In the morning, nothing had changed in our situation, but I felt different: lighter, as if my body was half its weight. I pulled on my sweats, went down to the hotel lobby to get a cup of coffee, and felt almost invisible. Although it was before seven, the seating area around the breakfast buffet was packed. Every table was filled with people talking, mostly, it seemed, about their escape from the flood or what they planned to do next. As I slowly stirred cream and sugar in my coffee, I stood by the counter, listening. No one seemed to notice I was there.

Everyone has a story, I thought. Some were full of faith, including the woman whose character would not permit her to abandon the family cat. She stayed behind on a tiny island of dry land until a helicopter could rescue them both. Others spoke of unity, where hundreds of volunteers worked through a day or night to sandbag a home in an attempt to save it from destruction. Still more shone with the purity of trust, as they laid their personal comfort and lives in the hands of total strangers who took them in after National Guardsmen evacuated them.

I quietly retreated back to our room, thinking about what I'd just seen and heard. *Character, unity, trust . . .* I'd seen them all before, in the hundreds of real-life stories I gathered for my writings, workshops, and lectures. Until that moment, it never occurred to me that there might be something more inspiring than the stories themselves. It wasn't just a matter of saving a cat or sandbagging a house. Instead, I had the feeling that the peace I craved lay in the discovery of some divine force that motivated these people to their life-enhancing actions while keeping their fear at bay.

I thought, too, of all the lessons I'd learned in the hundreds of books I'd read on motivation, creativity, spirituality, and metaphysics. *Everything starts as a thought. . . . Your feelings determine what kind of experiences you will have, as energy is attracted to that which is like itself. . . . Your life experiences are a result of your attentions, intentions, and beliefs. . . .* Somehow the people I was observing were able to sustain a peace of mind and heart that was making things go their way. How did they do that under these conditions?

As the weeks went by, I heard more and more stories. The people who seemed to be the most comfortable and unconcerned—in other words, the most peaceful—were those who used a combination of spiritual qualities to frame their thoughts, beliefs, and actions.

"I worked so hard, I slept right through the sirens and bullhorns!" one man roared, totally unconcerned with the danger he faced. It was obvious that his peace came from somewhere deep in his character. He had poured all his physical and mental energy into being a tireless sandbagger, which kept him from fear.

"Our house is a goner," another woman said, "but there were so many people who tried to help us save it, right up to the last minute. I wish I could thank them and tell them that even though we'll have to move, we'll be okay." Rather than dwelling on her loss, her attention was on blessing others with her gratitude and love.

I wanted both to tell the stories I was discovering and make better sense of them. I started by picking up the phone and calling every editor I could. Within forty-eight hours, I had an assignment from *Ladies' Home Journal* for the story of a woman who had lost both her home and her business in the flood. In spite of her losses, she was remarkably confident, and I knew that by interviewing and following her over the coming months, I would learn a great deal more about personal peace.

As the days and months went by, I observed some other common threads among the people who were recovering the fastest and the best. Not just from the flood itself, but also from the inevitable financial reversals, divorces, and illness that surfaced after the water retreated. I kept notes, comparing them to the real-life stories and the spiritual lessons I already knew. *These people have a gift*, I thought. Then I looked again. *No, not a gift. More than one. . . .*

And it wasn't just tragedy that brought out the gifts. Sometimes it was opportunity, revealed in something like a letter to the editor from a reader challenging our city government to broaden its vision of what our town could be. Other times it was the most ordinary moments that made a gift shine, such as the time I could see the joy in the eyes of an elderly neighbor as he paused from the work of mucking out his basement so he could pet Lady, our collie. At that moment, what was probably the most horrible afternoon of his life was made sweeter by the simplicity of noticing the beauty of a pet. I soon discovered that the lessons of the flood were not about trying to hold back water but, rather, what it allowed us to unleash in ourselves.

THE GIFTS

In time, I could see that the most peaceful people actively used ten gifts. I made a small poster of them on my laptop computer, and put it up near the kitchen table in our temporary apartment, which I was using as my desk. Whenever things got tough, I'd look over at it and ask aloud, "Okay,

God, which one should I use for this?" I eventually discovered that there wasn't any situation that the gifts couldn't improve or correct. What was even better was how peaceful I felt when I used them.

So, rather than wait for more trouble, I started using my gifts proactively to take control of my life. The gifts became sources of safety in times of danger; the next step needed to move a dream forward; visions of love that opened my frightened heart to the beauty all around me, especially that in other people. Using my gifts delivered me not only to my newly emerging life but also to a better part of myself than I had ever known. The more I used my gifts, the more my restlessness, fear, and discontent started to disappear.

The best way to describe the gifts is to call them spiritual verbs, life-enhancing abilities given to each one of us at birth to create the outcomes we desire. In spite of their names, I do not consider them nouns. The results that are produced by using your gifts are certainly tangible, but the gifts themselves are unformed until we use decide how they are to be used and take action. You may doubt you have them, but I assure you that you do. If you were faced with trouble, you would set one or more of yours in motion. I noticed that some people use theirs all the time not only to benefit themselves but also to be of divine service to others.

The ten gifts are:

The gift of Faith, surrendering any problem or fear to a higher power. I call this loving resource God, but you may call our Creator another name. The gift of Faith answers the question *"What problem do I wish I could surrender to God?"* It enables us to release our doubts, resistance, and limitations without hesitation. This gift also can be used when no trouble is around, as it instantly creates possibilities far beyond the scope of our current experience. Used this way, it answers the question *"What's the most wonderful thing that could happen?"*

The gift of Love, expressing our tenderness and splendor

by noticing and helping to bring it out in others. The gift of Love answers the question *"What beauty do I see in the people and things around me?"* Although it can be expressed intimately with a lover, the gift of Love is better used to create something other than romance. It is the conscious choice to reveal the best in any other living being(s), whether another person or group of people, an animal (such as a pet) or a plant, a field, an ocean, or forest. Using the gift of Love eases our self-consciousness and delivers us to one another in ways that uplift all involved.

The gift of Dreams, cocreating with God by focusing on what inspires or uplifts us. This gift is unique to the human species, as we are the only life form capable of both forming a good intention and actually carrying it out. The gift of Dreams answers the question *"What would make me happy?"* It is God's way of constantly inventing new and better things here on Earth through us.

The gift of Courage, taking physical action toward the object or objectives of our love and dreams. This gift answers the question *"What am I willing to try?"* It is the gift that makes change fun and exciting rather than frightening. While the gifts of Love and Dreams launch the process of creation, the gift of Courage is the force needed to move things forward.

The gift of Unity, multiplying our gifts by one, two, a thousand, or ten million. This gift reminds us that we are not alone in our life quest here on Earth but, rather, part of a huge tribe known as the human family. This is the gift that will deliver you to what feels like your soul mates, like-minded spirits who will willingly join forces with you for the sake of a vision higher than any that could be accomplished alone.

This gift is often linked with the gift of Faith, for once a problem has been surrendered, the best possible person or team for its resolution often shows up"coincidentally" or "miraculously." The gift of Unity is our guarantee that we will have the strength and resources necessary to carry our gifts of Dreams and Courage forward to their best results, for the good of the whole. It answers the question *"Who can help me?"*

The gift of Joy, taking abundant pleasure from what we have created with our gifts. This gift qualifies the other nine, suggesting that we are not meant to use our gifts simply to survive but to satisfy our souls and to inspire others to do the same. It answers the question *"How can I best share or express my happiness?"*

The gift of Trust, connecting to our higher selves. This gift is the God-given internal radar system that aligns our thoughts and actions with the divine will for our ultimate growth and freedom. It helps us feel comfortable, both with ourselves and with other people. The gift of trust also keeps us safe, as it alerts us instantly by making us feel bad whenever we think, say, or do anything that could be harmful. It answers the question *"When do I feel good?"* because it is constantly guiding us toward people and situations that help us grow and be free.

The gift of Character, understanding who we are now and who we want to be in the future. This is the gift that reminds us that each of us is totally unique and necessary to the life of the world, which is why we're here. The gift of Character allows us to reinvent ourselves over and over throughout our lives. It keeps us in constant harmony with the expression of our other nine gifts, so that we are able to "walk our talk," as they say. It answers the question *"Who do I want to be now?"*

The gift of Thanks, blessing whatever we've created with our other nine gifts. In the book of Genesis, God acknowledges the beauty and perfection of his/her creation by saying "It is good." This is pure contentment, the ultimate peace. The gift of Thanks makes it possible for us to do the same and enjoy the same peace, if only for a short while. When we use this gift, we pour positive energy into the lives of others, making it easier for them to use their own gifts. The gift of Thanks answers the question *"Who or what can I bless?"*

The gift of Intention, the ability to choose a new direction or return to an old one, regardless of current circumstances. This gift makes it possible for us to leave the past behind or trade something good for something even better. It's the assurance that no matter what happens, "It ain't over till it's over." Intention allows us to start fresh or take a quantum leap forward at any time. It answers the questions *"What now? What next?"*

Since the flood, there has never been a day when I have not thought about or used the ten gifts. I often start my day by asking "Which gift will help me be my best today?" I use them daily to enhance my work and interactions with others, and see them expressed everywhere I go. I know without any doubt that they do not belong to a "worthy" few. You can't buy them at a church, temple, or mosque. There's nothing you need to do to "earn" them. They're already yours. The only thing you need to manifest them is desire, making a conscious choice to do so.

Weeks after we evacuated, my family and I went home. Miraculously, our house was still standing, and thanks to its position on a small hill, only its basement had flooded. We mucked out our lowest level, which had filled with seven and a half feet of poisoned water, and emptied our garage, which had taken on three feet of toxic sludge. Although we lost a great deal of personal property, we eventually felt redeemed, not burdened, by the whole experience. Much of what we had been saving was actually holding us back from creating more growth in our lives, and once rid of it, we found we had less to maintain, insure, or dispose of. Literally and figuratively, we were lighter, freer.

We also discovered the joys of Unity as we worked with our employees to reinvent our stores. We used our gifts of Love to see their magnificent strength of character, as they did everything in their power to make our Fargo operation profitable while reinventing the Grand Forks store to meet changing market conditions after it reopened. At a time when their own lives had serious challenges, they helped our third-generation family business recover.

Our daughters gained a new level of maturity and self-confidence from the experience, and Steve and I, liberated from old roles and beliefs, began pursuing our dreams—he in photography, me as a full-time writer, consultant, and speaker. I left my marketing position at the store and struck out on my own, something I would have been too afraid to do before the disaster.

Although our house withstood the flood, it is in the path of the proposed dike, so in 1998, Steve and I decided to voluntarily sell it to the city and move to a spacious town-home on the opposite end of town, far away from the river. Although our new place is architecturally simpler than our old one was, it is also a lot easier to own and maintain. And we were able to create one thing we never could in our pre–turn-of-the-century house: a full-size photography studio for Steve, one of his dreams come true. So when people say to us "What a shame; you lost your house," we add, "And started having more fun than we've had in years." More than anything else, we have learned to treasure our lives, each other, the people connected to us, and our work far more than any possessions in our care or any roles we play. So far, so good.

In April 1997 I wanted God to make me a miracle so I could calm down and feel better. At the time, I was thinking along the lines of something spectacular, such as rolling back the water or having someone deliver a suitcase full of cash to my hotel room with no strings attached. But now I understand that, indeed, God did make *me* a miracle. And you, too. God gave us life and the ten gifts. With them, we all have everything we need to create peace within ourselves and our world.

. . . .

Defining Peace

Jot down your answers to the following six questions, enter them in your computer, talk them over with a friend, or record them onto a cassette tape. You'll use them as a benchmark to gauge your progress as you experience the gifts, proof of your ever-increasing peacefulness. Your answers also will serve as a practical guide for you in your progress journey, giving you people, places, and circumstances you know you can count on to enhance or celebrate your emerging peacefulness.

1. Why do you want personal peace now? Try to go beyond answers like "Because I'm stressed to the max," which indicates little more than you want some immediate relief. Instead, ask yourself how you and your current life would be different if you were peaceful now. Would you experience more kindness? Have fewer headaches? Get married? Try a new job? Close your eyes and try to imagine what you are both giving up and getting by becoming peaceful.

2. What do you think personal peace feels like? If you can find the feeling by closing your eyes and calming your current level of fear or discontent, fine. But chances are, you'll need a reference point. Try reaching into the past, making note of any setting, sound, texture, aroma, or flavor, if any, of a peaceful moment you remember. In other words, if you always felt peaceful at your grandmother's house, replay your memories of how her house looked, sounded, and felt, and see if you can remember how you acted, including what you thought about and/or said to others. In other words, bring it back to life in your mind. Here's an example:

Sitting in the living room of my grandmother's house was like taking a warm, pink bath. . . . She liked pink roses, hung pink curtains, and had a Victorian loveseat made of real cherrywood with a dusty pink velvet cushion that was overstuffed with goosedown. When I sat on that loveseat, the cushion would puff up around me and I would disappear in its cleavage . . . and as I sat there, my little legs swinging, unable to reach the floor, I could smell a pan of her famous brownies baking in her old, white enamel oven. . . . I could hear my parents and my aunts and uncles laughing on the sun porch at something they saw on television, and I remember asking my brothers and my cousins if they wanted to go up into the attic after supper and dig around in Nanny's big steamer trunk full of yarn. I was excited when they said yes, because I was too young to be allowed to go up there alone to treasure hunt, and because I knew Nanny would knit me a new scarf, sweater, or hat, depending on how much matching yarn I could find. . . . and I remember feeling happy and ready for some fun. . . .

Or try to get a sense of the feeling by thinking of something that makes you feel relatively safe and comfortable now, including sleeping in your own bed, stroking a pet, or listening to your favorite music. Again, you can write, think, or speak your impressions out loud.

3. *When do you feel most peaceful in your current life?* Although your immediate reaction may be to say "Never!" if you give yourself thirty to sixty seconds to think about it, you'll probably come up with a time of the day, week, or month that is relatively painless for you. Maybe it's the moments just before you fall asleep, or when your toddler cuddles up beside you to take a nap on a Saturday afternoon. Perhaps it comes after you've paid a few bills or cooked an especially good dinner. The peace might come in prayer, while reading, or when you're staring out the window on

your commute to work. Another way to approach this is to ask yourself "When am I the least annoyed or upset?"

4. *Who makes you feel peaceful?* It could be anyone from today's circle of family, friends, coworkers, or acquaintances, or it could be people from your past, even those who are deceased. If there's no one in your life experience who has ever made you feel peaceful, try to imagine meeting someone who will. Again, it's helpful to go beyond a mere list of names to noting one or two reasons why these individuals make you feel peaceful. Here are some more examples:

Uncle Eddie, because he makes me laugh. . . . Rocky, our miniature Schnauzer, because he'll sit quietly on my lap and let me pet him while I watch TV. . . . Mom, because she makes me warm milk and stays up to talk to me in the middle of the night. . . . Dad, because he likes to play and have fun. . . .

Again, if you're feeling negatively, a different way to approach this is to ask yourself "Who doesn't upset me too much?"

5. *Where do you go to find peace in your current life?* If the answer "nowhere" pops up, think again. We all have special places that feel right to us. It doesn't have to be a retreat-type space, such as your bedroom or a secluded beach in the Caribbean. Think of peace in terms of non-resistance, when you experience the least number of negative thoughts.

It might be when you're working on a hobby and lose track of time or when you're actively involved in caring for your family, your garden, or your pet. When I was a girl, it was lying at the top of the one hill in Echo Lake Park, which was not far from my house. There I'd lie on my back and make pictures out of cloud formations, an activity that could go on for hours. Now I have a large, hunter-green velvet wing chair in our living room that I use for meditation.

When I sit in it, I know I will feel peaceful, even when I'm not meditating. It's comfy and sturdy, and when I sit in it, I feel safe.

6. *How will you know when you've achieved peacefulness? What do you imagine you will be like?* If this question seems too abstract, start looking for examples of other people who have some measure of peace in their lives. It might be your elderly neighbor down the hall who laughs off small stresses, or the coworker who's just made it through a serious illness with her sense of humor intact.

If you don't know anyone who fits your definition of peacefulness, take a mental romp through history until you can think of someone who does. If you choose a religious figure such as Christ or the Buddha, be sure to ask yourself if you believe you can achieve similar results. Otherwise, all you're doing is creating conditions that ultimately will make you more stressed, not more peaceful. The point of this question is to help you fashion a definition of peacefulness that is right for you, not anyone else.

. . . .

CHAPTER TWO

The Gift of Faith

OF ALL OF the gifts, none is more critical to the pursuit of personal peacefulness than the gift of Faith. Many people think this gift is something that is obtained in the practice of a particular religion or set of rituals. That may be one way to find it, but blessedly, we all have the gift of Faith, whether we attend worship services or not. If you are non-religious and think you lack the gift of Faith, ask yourself: Where do things like inspiration, intuition, and conscience come from? What is the source of our feelings and emotions? While our DNA may have something to do with it, my thought is that since you have a soul, you have the gift of Faith.

The gift of Faith is one connection to our Source, although using this gift can be a problem, even for those of us who believe in a higher power. Most of us have been taught that our creator is up in heaven, over the rainbow, or perched on some sort of celestial throne we can only imagine. In spite of our divine seed, we wonder, "Does God really hear me when I pray?" Sure, we know God has the power we need, but He's like the fix-it man in the next state: You're on His list, but He's got bigger jobs to attend to first.

How are we supposed to learn to trust God, which is the basic definition of faith, if we're not absolutely sure if, when, or how God is going to respond?

FAITH IS NOT PATIENCE

We often hear people say "Have faith" when what they really mean is "Be patient." But the gift of Faith has nothing to do with patience. When you have a reason to use your gift of Faith, the last thing you want to hear or believe is that you're going to have to wait, possibly indefinitely, for results. If your husband has just walked out on you and your three kids, if your house was just blown apart in a tornado, or, if you just found out you have some deadly disease, you want things to change for the better as soon as possible. Right *now*.

The gift of Faith is not passive. Contrary to what most people believe, its purpose is not for you to wait *for* God but for God literally to wait *on* you: "Your order, ma'am?" There's a wonderful gospel song with a line that goes "Jesus is on the line, tell Him what you want . . ." Actually, telling God what you want is too hard for most people, mostly because we've been taught that it's selfish or wrong to do that. The other reason is that when you're using your gift of Faith, usually it's because the only thing you're aware of is something you *don't* want. But that's good, because that's exactly how the gift of Faith was designed to be used: to get rid of what you don't want or no longer need in your life.

FAITH AS SURRENDER

The gift of Faith comes alive when you consciously choose to surrender a problem to God. "Here, God. I've had enough of this misery/pain/frustration/doubt/fear. You take it." Just give it away. Hand it over. Be done it with it once and for all. Sounds easy, but it's not.

It's a fact that each of us produces 50,000 thoughts every day. This means that we have a new thought about every second and a half. Almost as soon as we form one thought, a new one is replacing it. This would not be a problem if each thought was more positive than the one before it, but that's not the case. The sad truth is that 80 percent of what we think is framed negatively. Our brains are bombarded with thoughts of what we *can't* do, what *isn't* going right, what we *don't* want to have happen, and what *won't* work. Sadder still is that fact that more than 90 percent of what we think is nothing more than a repeat of what we thought yesterday!

It doesn't matter how positive a person you are. We all have this negativity, as it is first and foremost a survival instinct. As human beings, we are motivated by two things: the avoidance of pain and the pursuit of pleasure. The avoidance of pain is the stronger instinct, which means that we evaluate every relationship and situation not in terms of the potential pleasure it may bring us but by how much pain we might suffer because of it. Although people in my workshops often ask me how they can lose their negativity, I remind them that we really don't want to. If we didn't have this built-in defense, we'd all be bungie-jumping off the Empire State Building and having intimate relationships with every person we meet.

The second reason for negativity is that it keeps us socialized. Although we say in America that we love winners, the truth is that we really hate them. We're quick to say "I feel your pain," but if a colleague comes waltzing into work saying that she lost twenty pounds, just received roses from her amazing lover, has the winning Powerball ticket in her purse, or just landed the biggest contract the company has on record, we're likely to grit our teeth, smile, and think "I *hate* her." The fact is, most conversations center on what is bothering us or going wrong in our lives. We call talking about the good stuff bragging, or arrogance. Misery is more socially acceptable.

If a friend asks you how you are and you start talking about everything that's going right in your life, her eyes will likely glaze over at some point and you'll get dull responses like "Uh-huh" or "That's nice." But if you confide a problem, she'll sit up, tune in, and start offering advice, sympathy, or inspiring examples of how she solved something similar in her own life. So if you really want to connect with people, find something that you're willing to be publicly unhappy about. Again, this is not entirely bad, as life would be pretty boring—and we'd never have a reason to use our gifts—if there was nothing to improve or fix in our lives.

The third reason for our negative thoughts is simply habit. I once read an article that said that by the time we're eighteen years old, we've heard the word "No!" approximately 144,000 times. (I once said that in one of my workshops, and a man raised his hand and said, "You never met my mother!") Again, the reason for this is to help us survive and be socialized. We tell our toddlers, *"Don't* plug your fingers in the electric outlet!" and "You *can't* yell at the movies." In school, we hear, "This *isn't* the time for that," and "We *won't* be able to go on a field trip." And, of course, teenagers make a career of acting out against what they *can't* or *aren't* supposed to do. Although our souls hate limitations, our bodies do better if we have a few. So again, the negativity is useful to us.

Is it any wonder, then, that our thoughts about God's availability to us are probably negative? Even if your soul is willing to give your problem to God, your brain is likely to override it, saying *Ha! Are you kidding? God* doesn't *want your puny messes! God* isn't *going to just take them away!* Can't *you think of anything better to try?*

FEEL PEACEFUL INSTANTLY

The good news is that the easiest and fastest way to use your gift of Faith is to dive headfirst into all that screaming, bubbling, rotten negativity that's hogging your thoughts. Tune in. Listen to it. Write down every nasty thing it says to you. Let it make you feel truly terrible. Stay with it until you just can't stand it any more. Remember that our number-one instinct is the avoidance of pain. There's a limit to how much you can take. So go ahead. Saturate yourself until you've had enough.

Sooner than later, I hope, you'll let go with a "Help!" or "Take this, already!" It doesn't matter how you phrase it, and you don't have to be down on your hands and knees asking. It's like the Hot Potato game we played as children. Someone tossed a hot baked potato to you, and the idea was to get rid of it by tossing it to someone else before you got burned. This is the same thing. Life handed you a burning problem. Hold onto it too long and you're going to get hurt. Pretend God is standing next to you in the circle and pass it over.

When you do this, you will be amazed at how you feel. In an instant, you will go from feeling as if you have an anvil cemented to your shoulders to feeling as if someone used a crane and lifted it off. You'll be able to take a deep breath. You'll feel as if you can wiggle your toes and snap your fingers. You'll smile or, at the very least, stop scowling or crying. In short, you'll feel better.

There were countless times during our evacuation when I used my gift of Faith. Whenever my fear for our future got too great, I'd say "Here, God!" and try to turn my attention to something else. Once I surrendered the problem, I figured the best way to demonstrate my faith was not to worry about it any more. It always worked. If the problem did resurface, it was usually in a form I was capable of handling.

When you use your gift of Faith, something wonderful

happens: You can get some sleep, eat a decent meal, or have a conversation without screaming or cowering in silence. You get your life back. If you've ever been in so much trouble that you don't see any way out, you'll know that relief *is* a miracle and, sometimes, can help produce one.

KATHY'S STORY

Three-year-old Josiah wasn't feeling well. He woke up vomiting, with a splitting headache. Kathy took her youngest son to the doctor, who said it was the flu, likely to go away in a few days. Although Kathy should have been reassured, something inside her made her ask "Could it be a brain tumor?"

When Josiah's "flu" didn't go away, a CT scan revealed that Josiah's problem was, indeed, a malignant tumor wrapped around his brain stem. Surgery removed almost two-thirds of it, but the prognosis was grim. Josiah had less than a 40 percent chance of survival. Josiah's doctors wanted to give him chemotherapy and radiation, but Kathy and her husband, Randy, said no. "According to everything we read, the treatments wouldn't help prolong his life by much," she says sadly. "And they would make him much, much sicker in the meantime. We decided to make whatever time he had left the best it could be."

Against their doctors' advice, Kathy and Randy decided on a controversial nontoxic treatment for Josiah. They traveled to Texas so Josiah could receive an experimental protein that was supposed to prevent his cancer cells from reproducing. Kathy and Randy had nowhere near the $60,000 it would cost for a year of the treatment, so they appealed to their community for help through a series of newspaper articles and donation cans placed around town. Before long almost $35,000 had been raised, enough to begin.

Josiah lived normally for about three months on the protein treatment but then developed a staph infection, which required him to quit the medicine. Within weeks his tumor grew precipitously, and he was dying. The doctors said there was nothing more they could do and that Josiah would likely be dead within a few weeks, before spring. So Kathy and Randy took him home, called Hospice and Make-a-Wish, and started to prepare their child to meet God.

"I would lie in bed with him at night and sing, 'Heaven Is a Wonderful Place,' " Kathy recalls. "One day the reporter who had been following the story came over. Josiah was so bloated from hydrocephalus and steroids that he was hardly recognizable. She turned to me with tears in her eyes and said, 'How can you stand it?' And before I could even think of an answer, Josiah looked up and started singing that song."

Buoyed by love and prayers, Josiah lived on. Not just weeks, but months. At his fourth birthday party in February, he said, "After I'm four, I turn five, right?"

"That's right," Kathy said. "You'll turn five in heaven."

Spring turned to summer. His doctors were amazed. "There's no way a child with this kind of pressure on his brain should be alive," they insisted. But he was.

In spite of their sadness, Kathy and Randy were determined to make something good come from their tragedy. First, they opened Josiah's Place, a coffeehouse and recreation center for teens in their town. Then they read about a little girl who needed a liver and asked their doctor if they could donate Josiah's. "Even though Josiah had had steroids, because he hadn't had chemotherapy or radiation, it was okay for us to donate his liver," Kathy says. She soon learned that the little girl's blood type was rare and that Josiah's was a perfect match. "We felt relieved," she said. "As sad as we were, it looked like our previous decisions had been the right ones."

Tragically, the little girl to whom Josiah was supposed to donate his liver died before he did. "I was angry," Kathy said. "I felt like I was on a rollercoaster. I said to God, 'I can't take any more of this!' I tried commanding God to heal my son, but I remember feeling really awful and could almost hear God saying 'Who are *you* to command *me*? Give him to me!' "

But Kathy and Randy wouldn't give up. "We went back to the doctor and asked if we could still donate his liver, and the answer was yes," she says. "But when the time came, they told us he would have to be airlifted from Beloit, where we lived, to Madison, where the hospital is capable of doing transplants."

One morning Kathy woke up with a premonition. "I heard a voice telling me to pack a bag and eat something, that I had to leave right away. I called the doctor, and she asked what symptoms he was having. When I said that he was sleeping and nothing had really changed, she wasn't fazed. Instead, she just said, 'Kathy, I trust your instincts; they haven't been wrong so far.' So we woke him up and went to the hospital."

Although Josiah was doing well when they arrived, by the next morning he was, indeed, near death. "At this point, I knew it was time to surrender my son to God," Kathy says tearfully. "I was tired. I couldn't take any more. It was time to let go." So Kathy and Randy, their other four children, and their extended family all gathered around to say good-bye. "Actually, we never said good-bye," Kathy says, her voice cracking with emotion. "We just said, 'See you soon.' I had accepted his death and watched the helicopter leave. As it took off, I thought, 'Good-bye, Josiah. It's finally over.' "

Medically, Josiah was nearly dead. The paramedics intubated him for the fifteen minute flight to Madison, where the transplant team was waiting. But by the time he arrived, Josiah was extremely alert, squeezing the doctors' fingers and responding visually to Winnie the Pooh. The waiting doctors did not know what to do, so they consulted the new pediatric neurosurgeon who had arrived at the medical center just two weeks before. He looked at Josiah's X rays and was willing to treat Josiah as a patient instead of a donor.

Kathy and Randy agreed to surgery, and in a series of operations, the neurosurgeon was able to remove 98 percent of Josiah's tumor. And this time Kathy and Randy agreed to chemotherapy and radiation as well. "At that time we felt peace in our hearts to go ahead with the doctor's suggestions," Kathy says. After more than thirty-five hours of surgery and four months in intensive care, Josiah was on the road to recovery. He was able to go home for Christmas, although he had to return to the hospital for more therapy. He had to learn to breathe on his own, walk, talk, and eat all over again.

Josiah celebrated his fifth birthday at home in Beloit, not in heaven. He turned six at home, too. As of this writing, he is cancer-free, living a normal life.

"We were always surrounded by love and prayer," Kathy says. "We are so thankful for that." Both she and Randy believe that Josiah has a special calling. "I believe that we are here as tools and that each of us has a purpose," she says. "I just watch as God uses Josiah to soften people's hearts and the story of his miracle to bring hope."

FAITH AS POSSIBILITY

What happens if you don't have dire problems right now and still want to use your gift of Faith? There is another way to do so. Instead of surrendering a problem to God, surrender a *possibility*. Using the gift of Faith this way helps you move forward in leaps and bounds rather than baby steps. It's a lot of fun and produces results that often outlast the original event by decades or even centuries.

Used this way, the gift of Faith is best summed up by the question "What's the most wonderful thing that could happen?" Faith as possibility has a relative in the gift of

Dreams but with one important difference: When we use faith to create possibility, we go beyond the limits of what our imaginations can dream to the wonder and delight of experiencing something bigger, better, and more beautiful than anything we have ever encountered before.

Using your gift of Faith to open up a treasure chest of possibilities is not for control freaks, however. If you want God as a partner, you'll have to allow for opportunities and outcomes that will likely arrive in a different form from what you expected or thought you wanted. There's a joke about a man whose town was threatened by a raging flood. His neighbor drove by and called, "Get in! The flood is coming!"

"God will rescue me," he said calmly as he sat on his porch.

A short time later the street was covered with water. Another friend came by, this time in a motorboat.

"Get in!" the friend called. "The flood is coming!"

"God will rescue me," the man replied, and stayed put.

Not long after that, the flood had claimed the first and second floors of the man's house. He climbed up onto the roof, and a helicopter came by.

"Get in!" the pilot called. "The flood is here!"

The man refused again. "God will rescue me," he said.

Not long after that, the man drowned. As he approached the Pearly Gates, he asked, "God, I had faith in you. Why didn't you rescue me?"

"I tried!" God answered. "I sent you a car, a boat, and a helicopter."

So if you want to use your gift of Faith, let God handle the details. Forget logic: It will play little or no part in what eventually happens. Just know and trust that things will work out perfectly.

FIND THE FEELING YOU WANT

The process works pretty much the same way as surrendering a problem, except that you enhance your good feelings, rather than your bad ones, to jump-start the process. Start by thinking of something you'd like to have. It could be a job, a mate, a new car, a baby—anything you want. Once you have that in mind, forget the details of how you're going to get it, because if you knew those, you'd already have what you wanted. Instead, just sit or walk about or start talking about how you're going to feel when you *have* it. Note that I said how you're going to *feel,* not how you're going to get it. Remember that you're going for something you haven't yet experienced, something bigger and better than anything you've ever known. If you start trying to figure things out, you're not using your gift of Faith.

Keep thinking about that feeling until it starts to grow inside you. You might find yourself smiling, or experiencing a little lift in your step, or laughing as you speak. Just let the good grow.

Again, this might be harder than you think, because of the number of negative thoughts that will rush in to protect you from possible harm. And when they do, they bring doubt and its brother, disappointment, with them. Both dampen the effectiveness of your gift of Faith, so you'll want to get rid of them as quickly as possible.

Here's what can happen. Remember that we produce a new thought about every second and a half. So there you are, on a roll, enjoying feeling after happy feeling until about the fifth one. That's when those nasty negatives will start creeping back to protect you. Here's an example: *I'd love to have a job where I could work with animals. . . . I can feel one now as I pet his soft, furry head and look into his trusting dark eyes . . . and I feel happy as I see him romping about and playing. . . . we're outside on a beautiful spring day . . . but I'd have to go back to school to learn what I* don't *know and then* I wouldn't *have enough money to pay the rent and I* don't *really want to start studying again and there are* no *jobs around here like that. . . .* See?

If you want to use your gift of Faith to create a possibility, here's what I do: Either give it to God before you drift off to sleep, or get ready to bombard your brain with good feelings. If you give it to God as you drift off to sleep, your logical mind will move out of the way, at least for a few hours. But if you want to be more of an active participant, try thinking or writing approximately sixty reasons why you'll feel great when this possibility becomes reality. The reason for sixty is because this will take you about a minute to read out loud, enough time to get a good feeling going and keep it going, overriding those initial negatives. You can frame your positive feelings in the form of a prayer, but you don't need to. God will get it, either way.

The important thing is to stay true to the feeling, which should make you feel good—peaceful—rather than nervous or overly excited. If you start feeling anxious, it simply means that you may be confused or conflicted about what you want or have doubts that you can or will have it. Usually this happens because you're thinking logically, not using your gift of Faith. Just remember to feel good, and keep enhancing that good feeling. Or release the feeling and forget about it, either by distracting yourself or by going to sleep.

Then, when you're feeling really, really good, say to God, "Okay—take it!" Then what I like to do is imagine all kinds of amazing fireworks overhead, as if God were expanding and exploding it into something really appealing for everyone to enjoy. Your imagination will likely work in different ways, but no matter what, you should feel good.

This is when the fun comes in. Depending on the intensity of your positive emotion, your possibility may take more or less time to manifest. The more intense your feelings of peaceful pleasure, the faster your new creation will come. But don't expect it to arrive in any particular form, because

I can practically guarantee that it will show up in a way you don't expect. Again, remember that you can imagine only what you've already experienced, and what you want here is something bigger and better than anything you've ever known. That's why it's critical to keep your focus on *feeling good*, not thinking positive thoughts about a specific outcome. If you think of how something is going to happen, you'll also dredge up a hundred reasons why it can't, which renders your gift of Faith ineffective. But if you simply feel good and keep on feeling good, there's no resistance to block the attraction of what you want.

Here's what can happen when you use Faith as possibility.

THE VICTORY STORY

As the summer of 1997 progressed, it became obvious that even though we had all survived the flood, growing numbers of people in the Greater Grand Forks area would not be able to recover from the devastation without substantial help. Less than 10 percent of the population had flood insurance, and even those who did found the repair and replacement of basic necessities such as electrical panels, furnaces, and wells beyond their financial means. Although the U.S. government, relief groups of all kinds, and tens of thousands of volunteers came to our area to help, desperate souls who had exhausted all available resources began to turn to their churches for financial and other assistance.

The clergy were already overwhelmed trying to repair the damage both to their houses of worship and to their own homes. Still, they would not turn their backs on those in need, and therefore they got together to form a coalition to help those who "fell between the cracks."

Because our congregation is too small to have a rabbi, I represented the synagogue. At the first meeting I attended, the group was still trying to find a name and mission. We knew there were a lot of people who needed help, but how would we find them? What were we supposed to do for them? How could we be sure that our help was really their last resort, and how would we prevent fraud?

If not knowing our name or our purpose wasn't bad enough, we didn't have an office, a telephone, or a nickel to spend. So we prayed together, a jambalaya of Jews and Christians all reaching to God for one purpose: to help those who truly couldn't help themselves. "Bring them to us, God," we asked, "and make us strong."

Within a few weeks, the coalition had a name: VICtoRY, the Valley Interfaith Coalition to RecoverY. And we had an office, in one of the few downtown buildings that had reopened since the flood. Then the phone was hooked up, and began ringing . . . and ringing.

You have to be careful what you pray for, because you're going to get it. I was reminded of the story of a preacher who had a congregation of farmers. They needed rain desperately, or the year's crop would be lost. "Go home and pray for rain," he instructed, and the people did.

But when they returned to church the following Sunday, the preacher was enraged. "Everybody go home!" he thundered.

"Why?" his astonished congregants asked.

"Because you do not believe!" he insisted.

"But we prayed for rain all week," they wailed.

He leaned forward heavily on the pulpit. "Then where are your umbrellas?"

Callers to VICtoRY were begging for everything from a new outdoor deck to shoes for their children. A door-to-door survey of 10,000 homes only made us more confused. The established social services agencies became critical, saying VICtoRY didn't know what it was doing and had no business "competing" with them.

Worse, we barely had enough money to pay the rent and

the phone bill. Although donations were rolling in to the churches and the synagogue, they were earmarked for building repair, not support of individuals within the community. Plus, we agreed that the people needing our help didn't have to come from any of our congregations or be affiliated with any congregation at all, for that matter. When we went to hire an executive director and a grant writer, we wondered where the money was going to come from to pay their salaries.

Again we prayed. "Help us to be clear in our mission, God." That prayer helped us endure the doubts and frustrations of relief workers from the other agencies as we worked to try to find our place in the pecking order. Within a few months VICtoRY had its role: to take care of those who had passed the scrutiny of the social service agencies for need but had either exhausted all available financial and service options of fell between the cracks of eligibility.

We no longer went seeking those in trouble. As we had asked God, they were delivered to us at precisely the right time. The mayor recognized our efforts and began forwarding some checks from well-wishers that had been sent to the city for the "general recovery" fund. We had grants in progress, but it would take months before the monies would arrive. In the meantime, we had hundreds of volunteer laborers to feed and materials to buy to fix the houses of those too poor to do it themselves.

We opened and closed each meeting in prayer. Sometimes we simply asked to be less exhausted or more patient. Other times we just sat silent, unsure of what to ask for. But one day, just before we opened in prayer, I noticed a sign that the executive director had put on his bulletin board: "Trust me, Terry. I have everything under control." It was signed "God."

So I turned to the treasurer and asked, "How much do we need?" And he said, "A hundred thousand dollars should do it." I looked at the president and said, "Then I think we should ask God for $100,000." And we did—feeling a little selfish, but reminding ourselves that it wasn't for us but for those in need.

By our next meeting, we'd received several donations of $25,000 or more, and more money was arriving daily. But as the money rolled in, so did the requests for help. A grandmother trying to raise her daughter's five children had no clothes for them and no money to pay for a circuit breaker board. A farmer who had suffered three years of crop failure had no running water, as the flood had destroyed both his well and septic system. There were families who needed to restore apartments in their basements because the rent was all they had for income, and without that rent, they were ineligible for loans. It was obvious that $100,000 wasn't going to be enough.

Again we prayed. But this time, finally, we were ready to use our gifts of Faith as they truly were meant to be used. We asked God to bring us *all* the money and help we needed to do *all* the work that was ours to do. We admitted that we were ready for the most wonderful, the most amazing thing to happen for all concerned, and we were ready to accept all the good God would bring to us and work through us. No qualifications. No boundaries. Just "Go for it, God."

We originally thought VICtoRY might not make it one year. But within two years, almost *$2 million* had arrived or was promised. More than 565 families had been helped. The largest donation came from an anonymous donor—$1 million cash, with a promise of an additional $1.5 million in matching funds. And more money was promised, enough to help virtually every family whose case file had landed in VICtoRY's office. In addition, we booked more than 17,000 hotel room nights for volunteers from across the country. The thank-you letters read at the annual meeting were heartwarming, and the sense of well-being and peace in the room that night was profound.

Eventually VICtoRY's job in flood recovery will end. The

last nickel will be spent, the telephone will be disconnected, and the doors will close. But the positive effects of the interfaith collaboration will linger long after all traces of the organization disappear. People were fed, clothed, and housed who might otherwise be wallowing in misery for years to come. Friendships were made that will last a lifetime. Those of us who were involved stand ready to help interfaith coalitions in other disaster areas get up and running, to spare them our mistakes.

One of the things we will tell them is that they should use their gifts of Faith. For we learned that anything is possible, and God can't wait to help.

. . . .

Using Faith

If you feel ready to use your gift of Faith, try following these steps:

1. Take the phone off the hook (or turn off your cell phone), close the door, and find a comfortable, straight-backed chair in which to sit. Place both feet flat on the floor; let your hands fall naturally to your thighs or the arms of the chair. Close your eyes, or soften your focus by staring at something that makes you feel peaceful, such as a candle, a flower, a picture of Christ or someone you love, a beloved pet. You can open the window to let in the sounds of nature or turn on some music, but ultimately, the fewer distractions, the better.

2. Let your thoughts come up at will. If you're using the gift to surrender a problem, most of these thoughts

will be negative to the point of being frightening. That's okay. Just let them build.

3. When you start to feel restless, tense, or terrified, you're ready to use your gift. You'll know when you've had enough. As soon as you reach that point, say aloud, "Here, God—take this!" Imagine yourself handing off the whole rotten mess. If you're a visual person, you might "see" yourself doing this in your imagination, perhaps wrapping up your trouble in a bundle labeled "Faith," but most people will simply feel lighter or better, as if their burdens have been lifted.

4. If you don't feel more peaceful instantly, try it again. Use phrases and images of your own choosing to intensify the painful feelings until they get to the point where you can't stand having them any more. Usually the reason people don't feel peaceful is that either they have not allowed the feeling to intensify to the point where they absolutely can't stand having it any longer, or they doubt God's willingness to take their pain away. If it's the latter, try imagining something other than a big bearded man in the sky for God. You might want to see a roaring fire that you can toss your problems into or a vast ocean that will swallow them up. Ask yourself, "What do I believe is big and strong enough to destroy this problem and these feelings forever?" That belief is your gift of Faith talking. Listen to it.

5. As soon as you're satisfied that God has taken away your problem, surrender to the divine will for something better to enter your life. You might want to confirm this with a simple prayer, such as "Thank you for helping me." Again, remember that this gift is your assurance that you're connected to something bigger than yourself. Take a moment to savor the pleasant feeling of having used it to improve your life.

6. If you are in a situation that makes it impossible for you to escape from trouble long enough to sit quietly

and exchange your fear with faith, you can use a one-word prayer, such as "HELP!" or "Take this NOW!" or, more quietly, "Thy will be done."

7. If you're using your gift to create possibilities, get quiet and, rather than letting your negative thoughts run amok, turn your attention to something that makes you feel good right here, right now. For example, it could be the quiet in the room, or the way the chair supports your body, or feeling satisfied because you've just eaten a good meal. If that doesn't work for you, focus your attention on a color, sound, smell, or texture that you associate with bigger and better things.

8. Again, let the feeling build and build. For some people, thinking of the word "Ahhh!" or allowing the sound of "Ahhh!" to escape from the mouth will dramatically heighten the feelings of pleasure and peace that your gift is producing. When you feel really, really good, release the feeling to God. If you feel so moved, end with words of thanks and praise.

9. You can also try other Faith releasers, such as taking a walk in nature or spending time with a newborn baby. For some people, seeing a towering skyscraper or drinking in the colors of a sunset reminds them that there is, indeed, greatness surrounding us. You may look to the Bible, the Torah, the Koran, or some other religious tome. Perhaps you get the spirit when you see food on your table night after night. You may want to dance, sing, or run until your heart pounds and your muscles tingle with life. You might head to the movies for inspiration or stay home and make love. Yet another way to find your gift of Faith is to appreciate something the Creator created through you, such as a painting, poem, journal entry, vegetable garden, child, or friendship. The idea here is that a gift metaphorically kept wrapped and sealed in a box is of no use or pleasure to you. Take it out. Use it. Enjoy!

I used my gift of Faith countless times during our evacuation and recovery, although that was not when I discovered it. I have been using it for years, and often write my prayers to God as part of the surrender process. I offer you this simple one, which I wrote in my journal to both surrender and create new possibilities during our evacuation. You are welcome to change it according to your own beliefs and religious traditions.

Protector, Friend . . .
Help me. Heal me.
I surrender my doubts and fears to you, for they
    limit me.
Take with them my worries of tomorrow and my
    regrets about yesterday.
Free me now,
For I am ready for something better,
Something bigger and far more wonderful than
    anything I have ever experienced.
I give you my willingness to be happy,
My faith in the promise of renewal,
And my pledge to enjoy the blessing of my life for
    my own sake and Yours.
I offer my whole life to Your loving will,
Believing that all I am now experiencing will come
    to good in the end.
Creator, thank You for this moment,
For the gift of Faith,
And for the love that sustains all life.
Amen.

CHAPTER THREE

The Gift of Love

WHEN YOU USED your gift of Faith, you probably felt lovingly connected to something "heavenly" or "out there." The next gift, the gift of Love, links you with a heavenly feeling right here on Earth.

The gift of Love has nothing to do with romance. Romance, as too many have learned, tends to fade over time. The gift of Love never pales and doesn't come with a set of actions expected of its host. Although the gift of Love certainly can be used by two lovers to deepen their connection, it can be used anywhere, anytime to bring you closer to the people and life around you, including children, coworkers, neighbors, friends, teachers, and even plants and animals.

Like everything else, our understanding of love is colored by the 80 percent of our thoughts that are negative. We say we *can't* live without it but that we're *not* getting enough. We feel that we *don't* have any more of it to give, that we *won't* be happy until it arrives in our lives. Our popular music tells us that we can't buy it, that it hurts, that it's over too soon, and that it won't arrive on time. We hear such expressions as "Love makes the world go round" and that love "is more precious than gold," but the way we've defined it until now, love is like an earthquake—unpredictable, and likely to cause some serious damage in our lives. Love makes us both giddy and depressed, clear and confused, energized and defeated. Considering this, it's easy to shake our fists at God and ask, "You call this a gift?"

But the gift of Love defies the definitions and experiences we've long associated with the word "love." It is a gift of great beauty, the one that, above all the others, shows us how precious and perfect life really is.

LOOKING FOR THE GOOD IN OTHERS

I discovered the gift of Love at the Salvation Army warehouse in Fargo, North Dakota. It was four weeks after we'd evacuated, and our neighborhood had just been opened for inspection. Steve and I had stopped by to pick up some cleaning supplies and bottled water before we headed north to check on our house and, we hoped, start scrubbing.

The warehouse was teeming with activity. Dozens of people were touring the makeshift aisles, each with a Salvation Army volunteer who was helping fill their grocery carts with essential items—toilet paper, soap, toothpaste, canned food. There was clothing of every conceivable size, color, and type; rags, mops, buckets, and enough gallons of bleach to disinfect a small country; and goodies like toys for the children and motivational books from prominent speakers. From the back of the warehouse came the constant beeping of pallet loaders stacking mountains of diapers, dogfood, towels, sheets, and blankets. Everything had been donated from well-wishers all over the country, and it was all free for the asking.

When it was Steve's and my turn to "shop," the volunteer greeted us brightly. "Happy to help you!" she exclaimed with a smile. "Where should we begin?"

"All we need is a bucket and some cleaning supplies," I replied. "And some bottled water."

She started laughing. "What? That's all? Oh, no—we can do much, much better than that!" And with that, she became the consummate salesperson, pointing out box after box of available goods. We kept refusing her offers, and I noticed that she seemed to be somewhat frustrated by our unwillingness to take more. So when she showed us paper cups for chili and soup, I took them and said thanks. Even though I was feeling somewhat self-conscious, when she threw in some paper napkins and spoons, I commented on her thoughtfulness. And when she added toilet bowl cleaner, dish detergent, and window cleaner to our cart, I forgot about my fears for a moment and instead raved about her generosity. She responded by saying, "Forget it. You have some big work in front of you. These things might make it a little easier. God bless." That's when I realized that I had missed the point. She was able to see the strength in us; I needed to see the good in her.

When we finished, I gave her a hug and thanked her again and noticed that she was smiling brightly once more. I then figured that a stop at the rest room was a good idea, especially since I knew there was still no running water any-where in Grand Forks. When I stepped inside, there was a young girl—maybe eleven or twelve years old—who was sobbing in the arms of her mother. Although I didn't want to embarrass them with my attention, it was impossible not to notice the girl's misery and want to respond to it. I asked the mother what was wrong.

"The flood took our house—we watched it go under. We've lost everything. Now my daughter thinks we're poor."

I nodded and swallowed my stomach, which was fast making its way toward my throat. I had no idea of the fate of our house. Steve had been the last to leave, and he had barely made it out, as the water was pouring down the street as he pulled away. What would we find when we unlocked the door?

Still, I knew I wanted to—needed to—say something to this frightened child, for her sake, her beleaguered mother's and mine. I felt awkward, uncertain. What could I say to reassure her? How could I help take her mind off her problem and direct her attention toward a solution?

I touched the mother's arm gently. "May I speak to her?" I asked.

"Go ahead," she said. "I'll try anything."

I squatted down so I could try to look the girl in the eye. I knew my intentions were good; now I just had to try to find some soothing words. Then I remembered what I had just experienced moments before.

"Listen," I said a little tentatively, "you're not poor. In fact, right now you're very, very rich."

She peeled her gaze from the floor and glanced up at me. I cleared my throat, hoping that what I was about to say next would come out right.

"You know why? Because right now, you have something that all those people out there who are trying to help us want."

She stopped sobbing.

"You see, all of those people out there came here to help us," I said, feeling a little more certain. "They want us to feel better, but they also want to feel good about themselves. And they can't do that without us."

She sniffled but didn't say anything.

The words began to flow. "They're here because they want to give us their love. But you know what? If we don't take it, if we say things like 'No, thanks, I don't need want your help,' then they've got nothing. And then *they* feel really poor because it's like what they have to give isn't worth anything to us. They haven't given us a gift because we haven't accepted it. It's only a gift if we take what they're offering and say thanks. Does that make sense?"

I was nodding. She nodded, too. Then the motivator in me took over.

"So here's the deal. You go back out there with your head held high and smile at the next person who tries to help you. And when you take whatever they're trying to give you, you say, 'thank you,' and mean it. Because then you're even. They've given you something, and you've given them something back. But what you're really giving each other is something more precious than money or stuff. You're telling them that what they're doing is valuable and that you see the good in them."

Her mother smiled at me.

"And you know what? There's another way you're rich. You have to remember what you're receiving today. Because some day, when someone else is in trouble, God is going to tap you on the shoulder and say 'Remember in 1997, when I gave you everything you needed? Now you have to pay it back. Go out and look for the good in somebody else, and do something about it.'"

The girl smiled slightly. The mother thanked me, and when I left, they were still hugging.

WHAT BEAUTY DO YOU SEE?

That's when I knew I had discovered the gift of Love. It answers the question. "What beauty do I see in others?" For as I experienced that gray, early-spring day, the gift of Love is the recognition that people are beautiful *as they are.* It's not unlike the way we feel when we first experience romantic love, when the sky seems bluer and music is so sweet it makes us cry with joy. But the difference is that instead of love being an emotional rush, we *get* from another person, it is a gift we discover by *giving* our full attention and awareness to what is good, right, or potentially joyful in another person.

The Babemba tribe of South Africa are experts at using

their gifts of Love. If one of them acts badly, he is placed in the center of the village. All works stops, and every man, woman, and child gathers, creating a large circle around the individual. Then they begin to address him, telling him and everyone in the circle about all the good things that individual has done in his life. All of his good deeds and strengths are recounted. No one is allowed to exaggerate or falsify their stories, nor is anyone allowed to be sarcastic. Sometimes this tribal ceremony can last for days, until every last positive comment is shared. When it is over, a huge celebration occurs, and the individual returns to his tribal life.

The gift of Love is our ability to see beneath the surface, looking beyond someone's physical appearance or behavior to the longing of his or her heart. This can be challenging when devastating circumstances, such as illness or financial reversal, make someone ill tempered or behave in unkind ways. But that's exactly when it can be most satisfying to use, both for you and the recipient. On the other hand, you can use your gift of Love simply because you want to, not because anything is wrong. Used this way, the gift of Love makes us completely unselfconscious. It eliminates both expectation and fear, the twin butchers of relationships. Instead, using our gift of Love makes us forget what we think we want and reminds us that what we have before us now is perfect.

When you use your gift of Love, you will never be disappointed. What you'll find is that it makes every encounter much more fun, because there's always an element of surprise—make that delight—in it. If you can see beyond people's suffering to their strengths, it gives them hope. If you enter a conversation believing that you will enjoy it, you'll relax and be able to draw more beauty from what the other person is trying to say. If you embrace to give away your comfort, you and the other person will feel better. No matter how well you think you know someone, there's always something new to discover about him or her, as life challenges and changes us day by day. Finally, you can use your gift of Love to notice and respond to other people's gifts, too.

Here's what happened to one father who did just that.

GREG'S STORY

The sun sparkled on the freshly fallen snow that December morning, beckoning me to come outside and play.

I tiptoed into my daughters' bedrooms. Amanda, age thirteen, pulled the covers over her head when I suggested that we go sledding in the park. But Erica, then ten, was up for some fun.

By the time we got to the Lincoln Park dike, the one-and-only true sledding hill in town, it was packed with people. We paused at the top, where the dike met the golf course, the only other incline in the area. We watched as dozens of children and teens went shrieking down the icy slope. Next to us, a tall, lanky man was getting ready to launch his son. The boy looked to be about three years old. He was wearing a grin from ear to ear and bright pink cheeks that said they had been out playing for a while.

"Come on, Daddy! Let's go! Let's go!" the boy called.

The father looked over at us. "Okay if we go first?"

I couldn't imagine holding this gleeful child back a moment longer. "Sure—go ahead. We'll follow you."

So the father gave his son's sled a push, and off he flew. The boy shrieked with delight. But as soon as the father let go, he immediately ran after the boy and his craft. "He must be trying to keep him from bumping into other people," I said to Erica. "Probably a good idea, considering that the hill is so crowded."

We snuggled up on our own sled, with me in the back, holding on to my young daughter for dear life. The hill looked much steeper than I remembered from those in my own childhood, and there was an enormous elm tree at the bottom that looked threatening.

"Ready?" Erica called. "Get set, and . . ."

"Go!" I screamed as I scooted forward just enough to tip the sled over the precipice using my own weight. I closed my eyes, hoping the other sledders were watching us and somehow had the good common sense to get out of our way, since we had no way to steer our apple-green plastic dish. The icy air smacked against my face, in spite of the fact that I had it buried in Erica's back. The screams of the other sledders disappeared, replaced by the turbulent sound of the prairie wind rushing by.

We soared to the bottom of the hill in less than fifteen seconds, missing the giant elm by inches. When I opened my eyes, Erica was already out of the sled, jumping up and down.

"That was great, Mom! Let's do it again!"

I stood up, which was when I came to my senses. What rose before me was not a hill on a public golf course but Mount Everest. I realized that every time we flew down that hill, we would have to trudge our way back up the mountain, no easy task.

That's when I looked to my left. I saw the father pulling his son, still in the sled, back to the top. The boy was as enthusiastic as ever, and the father seemed relaxed, in spite of the climb.

"Hey, Mom—how about pulling *me* back up to the top?" Erica asked.

I could only laugh. "Are you kidding? I'll be lucky if I get my own butt back up there. I'm sure the only reason he's doing that is because he's afraid the boy's little legs will get tired."

By the time we got to the top, they were ready to go again. Over and over they repeated the same pattern: Father readies his son. Father launches his son. Father chases his son down the hill. Father pulls his son and sled up the hill. Boy cheers his father. They both laugh.

They did two runs to our one, every time. Their energy was extraordinary, although the father seemed to be having even a better time than his boy, if that was possible. They both had nonstop smiles. But there were two unusual things about the scene. First, the father never said "Let's rest a minute," and second, the boy never got out of the sled—not at the top or the bottom of the hill.

I didn't think anything of this until noon approached and the crowd started to thin out as they headed home for lunch. Finally it got down to Erica and me, the father and his son, and a small handful of others. But in spite of the fact that the crowd had thinned, the father still chased the sled and pulled his son back up to the top. "He can't be thinking the boy is going to crash into anybody," I whispered to Erica. "There's hardly anybody here."

I couldn't stand it. I wanted to tell him that he was an indulgent fool and to let the child pull his own weight once in a while. But instead I called over, "You have incredible energy!"

He paused from the action just long enough to answer me. "He has cerebral palsy. He can't walk."

I was struck dumb. In my wildest imagination, I couldn't imagine that this boisterous child had any kind of disability or illness. I was so inspired by the scene that I reported it in my newspaper column the next week. Although I didn't know the man's name, either he recognized himself or someone else did, because within the week, I received this letter:

Dear Mrs. Silverman,

The energy you saw me expend on the hill that day is nothing compared to what my son Greg does

every day. To me, he's a true hero, and someday I hope
to be half the man he has already become.
Greg, Sr.

Enclosed was a picture of the boy in his wheelchair. He was smiling and crossing a bridge, seemingly by himself.

The father used his gift of Love to see his child's ability to have fun, not the disability that might prevent it. He was able to ignore what were likely the screams and aches of his own body to focus instead on the boy's joy and well-being. When I last saw them, the father joined his son on the sled, and they both were soaring down the hill.

The gift of Love makes diseases disappear, at least for the moment. It shows how big we are when life conspires to make us appear small. It reveals how beautiful we can be, if only we'd look. It proves that we are far richer than we may believe and as closely connected to others as our hearts desire.

The gift of Love is also useful when the beauty in others is buried deep behind a hard outer shell of anger, defensiveness, reluctance, or hurt. When people talk or behave badly, it's easy to believe that there is no good or beauty in them and that we're better off abandoning or forgetting about them. But with the gift of Love, we have the ability to see beyond appearances to what could be. Coupled with our gift of Faith, the gift of Love is a powerful catalyst for transformation when we say "I believe in you." Sometimes this is difficult to do for someone who has little or no faith in him- or herself. But when we make the challenging choice to use our gift of Love to see the good in someone who can't seem to see it in him- or herself, amazing things can happen.

Here's what happened when the curriculum assistant principal of a city high school used her gift of Love this way.

LOU'S STORY

Everyone in school knew about "Lou's Boys," the black athletes whom the principal personally mentored in academics, self-discipline, and social graces. She set and enforced strict standards, but they accepted them because everyone in school knew that Lou's Boys went on to college. Lou refused to accept any grade lower than a B, insisted that misbehaving anywhere was not acceptable, and personally chose all the classes and teachers for "her boys." In spite of the academic and emotional challenges that often cropped up, Lou loved her boys, and they loved her.

Lou had a couple of other rules, too: When her boys left her office, regardless of the content of the finished conversation, she and the student shared a hug. This was sometimes challenging, as Lou had crippling multiple sclerosis and was confined to a wheelchair. So when one of her six-foot-seven-inch athletes bent down, things could get a little clumsy. Her other rule is that all their best work was displayed on her office door. And there was never a day when that door was not completely covered.

Lou knew that mentoring worked. "All students deserve interested adults who rejoice with them when they are successful and help them when failure raises its ugly head," she said.

So, a few years ago when the school coach asked Lou to help with Michael,* a sophomore who showed great potential as a football player, she quickly agreed. On the surface, Michael was cheerful and outgoing, and everyone liked him. He was a clean-cut kid who almost seemed too slight to be a football player. He was doing fairly well in his course work, although his academics were not terribly demanding. "I thought that mentoring Michael would be a

---

*Names have been changed to protect students' privacy.

cinch," Lou says. "But nothing could have been further from the truth."

Michael sailed through his sophomore year, and by his junior year, colleges started trying to recruit him. He received inquiries from Syracuse, Vanderbilt, University of Mississippi, and even Harvard. But at the second home game of his junior year, trouble started. Lou watched in surprise as anger and frustration caused Michael to throw off his helmet and shoulder pads and stomp off to the locker room in the middle of the game after an argument with the coach. Michael rationalized his behavior, saying he was provoked by the coach's refusal to listen to him. The coach didn't buy it, however, and suspended him from the team.

Although Michael continued to work with and get hugs from Lou, after he was suspended from the team for the remainder of the fall season, his grades started to drop. He insisted he could bring them up, but it wasn't long before his temper flared again. He struck a girl who had taunted him, which caused him to be suspended from school for five days. His grades fell precipitously, and he flunked English. He was dangerously close to being disqualified from the football team because his grade point average was so low.

Lou never stopped believing in Michael, however. She stepped up the number of conferences she had with him and repeatedly told him she loved him. In spite of his escalating troubles, he responded in kind. "I didn't love the boy less for his actions, but I sure was concerned about him," she says.

Michael's temper wasn't the only challenge Lou faced. Because the young man acted out his anger, Lou's husband wanted her to stop mentoring him. Her response was unequivocal: "I didn't even consider it."

But things got worse before they got any better. One night after basketball practice, as a group of students was waiting for the activity bus, trouble flared again. After being taunted once more, Michael hit another girl. Although he could have been expelled for his actions, his school district sent him to the Alternative Learning Center, where he received counseling in addition to his academic program. Lou's interest and caring for him never flagged. While Michael was gone, Lou continued to receive his recruiting letters and kept herself informed of his progress through one of the guidance counselors. Michael was doing fine, Lou was told, and his grades were good.

Michael returned to school within nine weeks and assured Lou that he was doing well. They had several talks about his temper and how he was going to control it from then on. Michael ended his junior year "with the reputation of being both a hothead and a poor student," Lou remembers.

By the first semester of Michael's senior year, he was playing catch-up, retaking courses from his junior year in addition to the four he needed to meet graduation requirements. He had a total of six required courses and two electives while most of his friends had only two required courses left and were already working as teachers' aides.

Despite his challenging academic schedule, with Lou's constant support, Michael seemed to be doing well, both on and off the field. His teammates said he had the best arm on the team, and Michael broke the school rushing record that had stood for thirteen years. The recruiting offers continued to pour in from colleges and universities all over the nation. When Michael wasn't in class or on the field, he would show up at Lou's office, flash his trademark shy grin, and crash on her floor for a quick nap before the game. The improvement in both his attitude and his academic work was subtle but steady. Although his interim grades were below Lou's standards, with extra work he pulled off a 4.0 GPA by the end of that semester.

But then a new problem arose. To be eligible for the NCAA, Michael had to have a combined score of 68 on the ACT test. He fell far below that not once but twice. "I wish

I could have taken the test for him," Lou said, "but I couldn't."

In spite of repeated setbacks, Lou knew that her stead-fast support and encouragement was bringing out the best in Michael. He never said much, but it was obvious that he valued Lou's opinions and guidance, and heeded them.

"I send my boys inspirational things every week or so," she says. "One of them was 'Lessons for Life.' The day I sent that one was a game day. On game days we frequently called one of Michael's friends who had graduated the year before and was up north on a football scholarship. This graduate was also one of my boys. On that particular day, the friend was all excited, saying that he was 'going to the League' [NFL] after his junior year in college. I didn't think much of the idea, and made faces or shook my head as he talked. But Michael just looked at me and said quietly, 'Never step on someone's dreams.' That had been one of the 'Lessons for Life' I had sent him earlier that day."

Lou kept looking for the best in Michael, and eventually it seemed to surface more consistently than his doubts and fears. As his confidence grew, Michael's life took a turn for the better. "He had been struggling with Algebra 2, and I asked him if he wanted to drop it. At first he said yes, but then he said no, because he wasn't a quitter."

In the spring of his senior year, he was accepted at Methodist College. "He looked as if the world was lifted off his shoulders," Lou said. In the end, Michael "was thrilled with his grades the last term," Lou reports. "You should have seen the radiance of his smile!"

No matter who you are with or how things may appear for them, they have beauty waiting to be discovered. Use your gift of Love to find it, and you'll find your own.

. . . .

Through the Eyes of Love

To use your gift of Love, you must first suspend—at least temporarily—most of the beliefs and experiences you've had about love to this point. The easiest way to do that is simply to make the choice to use your gift, including why you want to use it. For example, you can simply think or say out loud "I want to use my gift of Love to see more of the good in other people." Take a moment to consider what that means to you.

Then think back, if you can, to a time when someone noticed the good in you. Maybe it was a coach who said "You can do it!" or a friend who refused to believe an untruthful rumor about you, saying "I know you're not like that." It might have been the kindergarten teacher who first taught you how to write your name and then praised you for it, or the parent who thanked you for your help with household chores. If your childhood was empty of such support, try to remember a time when you recognized your own beauty and told yourself "I can do this!"

Think of how you felt at these moments. Words like "happy," "excited" or "proud" might come to mind, but mostly, the point of this exercise is just to remind you of how great it feels to have someone notice the good in you. You undoubtedly felt more precious, more valuable—more beautiful. Contrast this feeling with other times when either you beat up on yourself—"I'm so stupid!"—or someone else let you know you disappointed him or her. Then you'll begin to see how important it is to discover and use your gift of Love consistently, both for your own sake as well as others'.

The simplest way to use your gift of Love is to look for the good in others. It is even easier if you know them well—if, for instance, the person you're looking at is your child, spouse, or close friend. Start by watching and truly listening to people when they speak. You'll undoubtedly pick up clues about what would bring out the joy in them. Then use your gift of Love to remind them of the talents, experience, or character qualities they have that ensure they can have what they want. Go beyond being a cheerleader to giving specific examples of times when you saw them use these traits. Bring those moments alive as vividly as you can, even to the point of acting them out again. Watch and love as the "Ah-ha!" light goes on in your beloved's eyes.

Another way to use your gift of Love is to accept help from someone else. Ironically, for most of us, accepting help from another person is what we call charity, not love. We associate the receipt of assistance with helplessness, failure, and shame, not beauty and joy. So try this:

Think of someone right now who is trying to help you. It doesn't matter whether you think you need the help or not. Remember, the gift of Love is ultimately not about you; it's about what your attention awakens in the people around you.

Now think about the person who is trying to help you. You might consider him or her a busybody or a pain in the neck. You might think of the person as arrogant, pushy, obnoxious, or well intentioned but misguided. After all, you don't need help! How dare he or she offend you with such an offer?

Now look beyond what the person is offering to *why* it is being offered. Again, at first you may think that this other person simply is trying to be an expert at solving other people's problems rather than dealing with his or her own. But ultimately, if you really think about it, you'll realize that most people offer help because they want to be useful, valuable, connected. They may be critical, but it is because they're trying to make something better, not worse.

It is important to note here that the gift of Love is *not* about gratitude, especially that which is expressed insincerely. If you truly feel embarrassed or upset by accepting someone else's help, *don't*.

But *do* acknowledge people's intentions, *especially if they are not immediately obvious.* Look beyond *what* they're trying to do to the motivation behind their offers, in other words, learn *why* they're trying to do it. Search for virtuous qualities such as thoughtfulness, generosity, kindness, or selflessness. Pay attention to skills they may be using or trying to use on your behalf, such as ability to cook, build, clean, create, organize, or lead. If you can, go further, hunting for less obvious skills such as listening or learning. If you know the person well, think of other times you saw him or her use talents for your betterment or to uplift someone else. These things are love in action.

Finally, acknowledge the good in the person who is trying to help you. If you feel comfortable accepting the help, say something like "It's just like you to offer to lead the way. This project really needs a good organizer. Thanks!" If you prefer not to receive the help, accept their gift with a response like "You know? I've seen you do some amazing cooking before. Remember the time when you . . . ?" Then tell the story. You can finish by saying "You made a big difference that night, and none of us will ever forget it. I appreciate you wanting to do it again for me right now— that's very generous of you. But I'd like to do it myself— you've inspired me!"

One last thought. If you're just saying the words, you're not using your gift of Love. Think about what they mean, both to you and to the person to whom you're trying to give them. In our society, we often give gifts that don't have much thought behind them. Remember that you're not handling a piece of plastic; you're holding the heart and soul of another human being.

Treasure it.

CHAPTER FOUR

. . . .

The Gift of Dreams

THE GIFTS OF Faith and Love turned your attention outside yourself, with the goal of helping you feel safe, both with God and other people. The rest of the gifts build on this foundation, so you can feel safe with yourself.

During the flood, the only thing I knew for sure was how I was thinking and feeling. Day to day, we never knew what to expect—what the river was or wasn't doing, what the city would or wouldn't allow, who was where or what was happening to them. It was impossible to predict the future, even one day in advance.

When trouble hits, that is often the case. In spite of the best medical diagnosis, a prognosis can be uncertain. When a spouse leaves or a car breaks down, it's hard to say what will happen next.

While using the gift of Faith is a good way to take the edge off feelings of pain and helplessness, that gift alone is not enough to restore a sense of well-being that brings personal peace. And while the gift of Love can make us feel better about ourselves and others, it doesn't change the circumstances we're in. That's where the gift of Dreams can help.

I discovered the gift of Dreams online, hunched over my laptop in our hotel room. Steve was working at our store, and we'd just put the girls on a plane to stay with my parents for the foreseeable future. I had nothing I had to do and nowhere I had to be, which was precisely the problem. I needed to transform my restless energy into something useful. So I e-mailed my friend and former editor Cathy.

"Who do you think might be interested in our story?" I asked.

She answered my question with more questions. What was I trying to accomplish? Who would benefit from knowing this? How would I resolve a story that had no foreseeable ending? As I thought about what she said, I realized that what happened next, or at all, would depend entirely on my own clarity about these and other questions I had swimming around in my brain. How could I expect an editor to see where I was going if I couldn't see it myself? What would my happiness look, sound, taste, smell, and feel like?

That's when I remembered John.

JOHN'S STORY

John was a struggling artist barely able to make ends meet. Besides himself, he had a wife, two children, and an assortment of chickens, goats, ducks, dogs, pheasants, and a rabbit to feed. Although he worked fourteen-hour days to turn out critically acclaimed canvases of people and animals, his artwork wasn't paying the bills.

So he thought about his dream come true. He already had several elements of it: his family's love, a restful lifestyle, and, most important, the artistic style he wanted. Nearing forty, he was prolific, with an energy that he said sprang from his desire to express God's creations on canvas. "There's a part of the picture where it paints itself," he told me. "Painting isn't something I do; it's something I believe in."

But there was a part of John's happiness that was incomplete. And when he dreamed about the total picture of his own life, he saw himself making his family financially comfortable. So he wondered, "How do I do that?"

He was struck with an unusual inspiration: to turn himself into a corporation and sell shares to investors. The idea wasn't entirely new: Patrons had supported artists in other ages and places, most notably the Medicis during the Renaissance. Even Michelangelo had a patron.

But John was not interested in handouts from people he knew. His dream was to earn his money, not have it gifted to him. So he came up with an ingenious plan: After deciding how much money he felt he needed to live on, he would divide that number by ten or more and sell shares in himself. As his works sold, his investors would recoup their money in proportion to the number of shares they owned. If there was a profit, it was theirs to keep, not John's. And if his sales fell short, he promised he would provide them with paintings equal in value to the amount they lost. The paintings would be appraised, so the investors were sure of getting their money's worth.

The dream worked well for three years. John had all the income he needed to live on, and the investors received either their money or paintings in return. But John grew restless: "I was spending so much time tending to the corporation, I didn't have enough time to paint," he said. It was time to amend the dream.

This time, his happiness included a lot of other people. Not just their money, but their smiles and delight as they viewed his paintings and carried them off to their homes and offices. He called together old family friends, who instantly organized themselves into a volunteer committee to sell John's art. They decided to stay away from traditional galleries, as the commissions were too high. Instead, they started brainstorming other possible venues for a show of John's work. It was close to the holidays, and people would be getting together quite frequently. That inspired one of the committee members to offer his office, a stock brokerage, during the company Christmas party.

The party and the show were a huge success. More than five hundred people attended, and thousands of dollars worth of paintings were sold by committee members during the course of the evening. John made almost his full year's income in that one night and returned to his beloved family, animals, and canvases.

TEN QUESTIONS TO HELP YOU DECIDE

The gift of Dreams is the voice within us that knows that each of us has something special to give the world. Like snowflakes, no two of us are cut quite the same. Although our desires for things like a safe and comfortable place to live, people to love and who love us, and good health may be similar, how we envision those things varies significantly from person to person. If you ever found yourself wishing that everyone could be the same as you, think of how bored you would be talking, loving, working, or doing anything else with yourself. There would never be any surprise or delight, no challenge or way to move ahead.

But most of us have forgotten how to dream. I'm not referring to the kind of dreams you have while you're asleep—that's another subject entirely. Instead, I'm talking about the dreams you have while you're wide awake. The kind your teacher used to scold you for pursuing. The kind that think tanks pay for and most bureaucracies ignore.

These are the thoughts that lift you up, excite you, and give you a reason to get going in the morning. They are images of what you want to have happen, what you'd love to do or say or become. Some people refer to these as goals, but I don't. A goal is something you go for, and, thanks to the 80 percent of our thinking that's negative, most people never reach them. A goal is a single thing or moment. A dream is the big picture, a panorama of happiness that includes all kinds of subtleties that satisfy us both along the way and once we arrive. It's not just what we create; it's *how we are* as we are creating.

In addition, a dream, as opposed to a goal, is something that changes as we change. While you can always set new goals, goal-setting puts the focus on something outside ourselves. Dream-getting is the process of manifesting that which is life-enhancing within us. There can be many, many goals with a single dream, and achieving every one of them feels good, complete.

The gift of Dreams makes our creations not just possible but probable. It can be accessed by asking yourself these ten questions:

1. What would make me happy?

2. Why do I believe this makes me happy?

3. Why is this important to me now?

4. Who am I if I have this?

5. How do I act toward others when I have this?

6. How will other people benefit from this?

7. Who else do I know who has this (or a variation of it)?

8. Whom do I accept, forgive, or love in my dream?

9. When do I want this to happen?

10. Where do I end up as a result of my dream coming true?

These questions are elaborated at the end of this chapter. In the meantime, here's how one woman experienced her gift.

BECKY'S STORY

Becky was sitting at home on a Sunday afternoon, enjoying a good book, when she received a phone call from her husband. Without warning, he said he was divorcing her, which turned her life upside-down.

Her job as an office manager, which she had formerly seen as challenging, suddenly seemed overwhelming. Her finances took a hit, and she found herself wishing she could earn more money. Her younger daughter's grades dropped, and the older daughter refused to work and started taking drugs. The older daughter's behavior was so challenging that Becky finally had to ask her to move out.

Through all the commotion, Becky remembered to use her gift of Faith to stay calm and centered. Still, that alone wasn't enough to move her forward toward a new, better life, even though she knew that was what she wanted. She believed she could have that; she just didn't know how to get it.

That's when an editor at *New Woman* magazine contacted me to ask if I would like to work with Becky as part of a story on stress reduction they were doing. I jumped at the chance: I had used my own gift of Dreams during the flood to manifest bigger and better writing assignments and speaking engagements; now I could show someone else how to use hers.

Becky and I spent a lot of time on questions number 1 and 10. Eventually she described a scene to me where she was comfortably nestled in a mountain of rich red pillows on her oversized bed. At the foot of her bed was her beloved shihtzu, curled up and fast asleep. Beside her, on the nightstand, was a glass of icy cold milk fresh from five minutes in the freezer and a plate of warm chocolate chip cookies. There were two messages on her answering machine: one from her older daughter, saying that she found both a decent apartment and a job; and the other from her new love, a man who was committed to staying with her, saying he had found the perfect spot in the Caribbean for their honeymoon. Then her younger daughter walked into the bedroom to announce that she had just gotten an A on one of her midterm tests. At first, Becky saw herself reading the want ads for a new job, but later she decided she simply wanted to enjoy her current work experience more. Her happiness included a new love, thankfulness for her children's well-being, a few wonderful sensory experiences, and a feeling of being productive and satisfied with herself.

There was one other thing Becky wanted: an ever-deepening closeness to God. She wanted to use her faith as the foundation of her new happiness, and gave me some of the psalms that supported her belief that she had nothing to fear and everything to look forward to.

I took all of her descriptions and created a script of a scene in which Becky could see, hear, smell, taste, and feel the experiences that would help make her happiness come alive. I called and read it to her over the phone, to make sure the story I had written was consistent with what she wanted for herself. After she approved it, I taped it onto audiocassette with some gentle background music. Still, there was a problem: Although Becky knew what her happiness included, her worried, restless thoughts were constantly blocking its arrival. So I added a deep, full-body relaxation to the script, both to help relieve some of the stress she was feeling and to help her get comfortable with the idea of her dreams coming true.

THE KEY: LOWER YOUR RESISTANCE

The key to using your gift of Dreams is not a good imagination. Most of us can think of at least one thing we'd like to experience or create. Instead, the secret to making your dream come true is learning how to lower your resistance to having your dream. In other words, simply allow yourself to have it and be happy. This is extremely challenging for most people, as we think we have to struggle and suffer to make our dreams come true. That's because, as I mentioned earlier, by the time we are adults, we are imbued with our society's belief that it's somehow selfish or wrong to be happy and that nothing good comes easily.

The only way to change any belief is to have an experience that contradicts it. You'll need proof that everything—including you—can indeed be exactly the way you want it to be. Most of us can't change simply by thinking or talking about it with our rational minds. But it can and does happen quickly and easily when we are fully, deeply relaxed, and visualizing.

Some people open up through meditation or prayer. Others use a walk in the woods, soothing music, or deep breathing by candlelight. But I find that putting on a pair of headphones, closing my eyes, and listening to a precisely worded script brings my mental dream pictures to life better than anything else.

Becky did just that, listening to the story of her happy new life twice a day. I gave her instructions on how to keep a quick, easy journal, so she could see her progress in notes. And I'm happy to say that within several months, she manifested everything she had created with her gift of Dreams. Her older daughter quit taking drugs, got a good job, and a good apartment. The younger girl started doing better in school. Becky started enjoying her work much, much more, and laughed when she told me, "I'm the calmest person in the office! Now everyone wants to be around me." Best of all, she met and married a wonderful man. Today, her older daughter is happily married and, at the time of this writing, is about to have a baby. Her younger daughter is doing well at college.

The gift of Dreams is God's way of continually re-creating the world through us. Our misery does not serve God; our happiness does. I often think that the angels weep and God sighs every night one of us goes to bed feeling dissatisfied and unhappy. "Another day of life uncherished," they must say. We have been given bodies and minds, hearts and souls for a reason: to create our world anew day by day, month by month, year by year. In my religious tradition, Judaism, we are taught that every day is like a page in the book of our lives. I often shudder to think how many of my own pages I have left blank.

Embrace your dream. Live it in your mind, and then get ready, because it won't be long before you'll be living it out loud.

PEACE PROGRESS STEP 4

. . . .

Creating Dreams

The ten question that accompany the gift of Dreams are designed to help you identify and clarify the elements of your happiness.

1. What would make me happy?

Consider the whole of your life, not just one particular aspect of it (although you can certainly do the latter if the former seems too overwhelming). Do you have a mate? Children? A house, apartment, or boat? Do you like vacations? How healthy do you want to be? Is there music, mystery, adventure, romance in the picture, or is it simply a calmer, more settled image?

Try to look at some major life categories: family, friends, love, work, play, finances, health, politics, community, spirituality and/or intellectual growth. Think about each area separately, and jot down or talk out your thoughts about what you want to include in your happiness. You're also welcome to clip pictures from magazines, watch TV, or rent/go to movies to see how others incorporate these elements into their own lives. You do not have to include every category here, and you may certainly add other categories. Remember that there's no limit to happiness, so you may include as much or as little as you wish.

2. *Why do I believe this makes me happy?*

Go back over everything you've chosen, and test it against this question. If you can't come up with an answer that satisfies you, you may want to drop the category from the list or change what you want within it. Often what we think we want really isn't what we want at all. This question will help you go beneath the surface of things to the truth of what you really want, which is usually some form of freedom, growth, or joy.

3. *Why is this important to me now?*

This question will help you prioritize the categories. You'll want to concentrate first on creating the things that will be most satisfying to you now.

4. *Who am I if I have this?*

Close your eyes and see yourself thinking, speaking, and acting the way you know you will when your dream comes true. Then ask the question. See what you'll become. For example, you might be a wife, a pilot, a perpetual tourist, or a philanthropist. See what role you've created and if it feels right for you. If it does, continue. If not, review the previous questions. At one point, Becky saw herself as a paralegal working on Madison Avenue in

New York City. But when she asked herself this question, it didn't feel right, so she changed her picture to include a top-notch performance as an office manager for her present employer in Tennessee.

5. How do I act toward others when I have this?

If what you've chosen makes you funnier or more relaxed, compassionate, forgiving, or generous, you'll probably want to continue. If it makes you defensive, edgy, judgmental, or aloof, you may want to reconsider. Although some people say they want to be alone, I have yet to meet a single human being who wakes up in the morning and thinks, "Boy, I really can't wait to annoy or alienate someone today!" You don't have to strive to be the king or queen of popularity, but there's more peace in feeling comfortable around others than not.

6. How will other people benefit from this?

Once you know how you're getting along with others, see if what you've dreamed up helps them to grow or feel freer or more joyful in any way. If it does, you'll feel much more justified in making your dream come true and will gather enthusiasm for the experience.

7. Who else do I know who has this (or a variation of it)?

This will help you believe that what you want is possible. You can think of people you know, celebrities, historical characters, or even the deceased. You also can use this question to amend your dream, leaving out some of the mistakes you feel the other person has made. We learn best when we learn from one another.

8. Whom do I accept, forgive, or love in my dream?

I once read a spiritual piece that says that after we die, we get asked only one question. It's not "What did you accomplish in your lifetime?" Or even "How much did you help others?" Instead, the only thing God wants to know is "What did you learn about love?"

Make sure your dream moves you up the ladder of love in some way that's significant to you. And here's a hint: The person you accept, forgive, or love might be yourself.

9. When do I want this to happen?

Some people hate rapid change; others want things to change this very instant. Only you know what's right for you. Think of a few different scenarios, and see how they make you feel. Choose the one that you believe will work best for you. You always can amend your dream and change the timing of parts of it later, if you wish.

10. Where do I end up as a result of my dream coming true?

See your dream complete, with everything the way you want it to be. Use your five senses to make the picture come alive. Who is there with you? What are you thinking, saying, doing? What are you wearing? Where do you live? What are you eating or drinking? What do you see in terms of colors, textures, objects, light and/or darkness? What kinds of sounds or words do you hear? What aromas are in the air? Most important of all, how do you feel?

The answer to this question will become the basis for your visualization. Here's how to create yours.

VISUALIZING YOUR DREAM

Start with as much silence as you can create. Turn off the TV, stereo, and your cell phone. Take the regular phone off the hook or turn off the ringer. Close the windows, if street noises bother you, or open them if the outdoor sounds soothe and relax you. Turn off any other indoor machinery whose sound distracts you. Find a comfortable chair, one in which you can sit up straight. (Note: Yes, you can visualize lying down, but most people fall asleep before their dream is finished.)

Then take a deep breath. Breathe in through your nose, feeling the air build first in your abdomen, then lifting it up through your chest, neck, and throat until it lands behind your eyes. Hold for a moment, and then gently and slowly release the breath through pursed lips. Repeat three times.

Next, imagine that you are at the top of a soft, carpeted staircase. It can be indoors or out, as you desire. Count backward from ten to one very, very slowly, and as you do, imagine that you are descending into a place of great beauty.

Once you "arrive," see yourself getting comfortable. Then imagine that there is a ball of bright light over your head. It might look round and smooth, like a child's toy, or it might be a shimmer of radiant energy with no defined edges. Some people will not "see" anything but instead will experience the ball as a slight tingling or warmth in their scalp, as a sound of some kind, or smell it, as if it has an aroma. There is no right or wrong way to get a sense of the ball, as each of us processes information differently.

When you're ready, imagine that the ball is rolling through the curves and crevices of your brain. As it does, pretend that it acts like a celestial sponge that can soak up all of your cares and concerns, making them disappear. When your mind starts to quiet down, let the ball drop to the tiny muscles around your eyes, then through your sinuses. (Your breathing should open up.) Allow it to drop into your mouth and roll over your tongue and around your jaw.

Then feel it flow into your neck and throat and make its way toward your shoulders. Once there, allow it to split in two and roll down both your arms, into your wrists, hands, and fingertips. At this point, it's common to feel tingling or warmth in your hands. This is fine. In my workshops, I tell my participants, "It's just your blood circulation returning."

Then feel the two halves of the ball reconnect in the area around your heart and lungs, removing sounds of disappointment, frustration, and worry. Next it will drop to your stomach, settling it down, and then into your lower abdomen. Feel the ball split in two once again, and it will roll around your hips and to your lower back. Feel any discomfort, stress, or strain from sitting, walking, or lifting leave as it does this.

Then the two halves will roll down both legs simultaneously, past your thighs, knees, calves, ankles, and then into your feet and, finally, your toes. Again, you will likely feel a tingling when it reaches this point. It has absorbed all sounds of tension from your body and is ready to leave. Then hear it go, with a WHOOOOOSH!!!!! Relax and get a sense how good your silent, stress-free body feels.

Next, bring to mind the picture of your happiness, the answer to question 10. Make it come to life by imagining it in action. Pretend you're directing a movie, and set the scene, place the "actors," and think, "Action!" Watch it come to life. If you like, you can write this out as a script, and read it into onto a cassette. If you're really creative, you can include music and sound effects. Or you can have a friend or loved one read it to you from a sheet of paper or over the phone. You can improvise it, changing it a little bit every time. All of these techniques work.

Your "job" is simply to follow the storyline and allow yourself to enjoy every minute of it. The more you enjoy it, the more you believe it can and will come true, the more you welcome the feelings of having what you want, the faster it will occur. If you find yourself resisting any part of it, go back to the questions and clarify your desires. Otherwise, just sit back, relax, and enjoy!

Using your gift of Dreams this way comes with another very important benefit: improved health. Deep relaxation has been shown to lower your blood pressure, improve your heart rate, get rid of minor aches and pains, and boost immunity. So even if your dream is slow in coming, you're doing some very good things for yourself in the meantime.

Try to use your gift of Dreams every day, starting today, so that when you go to sleep tonight, God will smile, the angels will applaud, and you can think, "Thanks, all. It sure can be fun down here."

. . . .

CHAPTER FIVE

The Gift of Courage

DR. STEVE LEVINSON, in his book, *Following Through: Why We Can't, How You Can*, points out an interesting fact: There is no mechanism in the human brain for following through. In other words, we are capable of forming a good intention but have no biological assistance to make it happen. Levinson says that it's like riding in a car with two drivers. The first one knows where it wants to go, but as soon as a distraction arises, the second one says, "Oooooo! Let's go over there instead!"

This is why the gift of Courage is so important. We think we want to be brave and strong, which is how most of us define courage. But even though we might want to take on a bully or invest our life savings in the stock market, that "second driver" comes through loud and clear: "Are you kidding? Let's go watch some TV and eat gooey hot fudge sundaes instead!"

Most people associate courage with risk-taking, which is why we think we have so little of it. Very few of us eagerly embrace the unknown, as those who do often face tremendous struggle. Others define courage as facing your worst fear. Again, most of us are reluctant to do this, since we're biologically designed to avoid pain. While we may be inspired by those who define courage in these ways, we're not likely to choose to emulate them.

RESPOND TO YOUR HEART'S DESIRE

Instead, I discovered that the gift of Courage is actually something else: a simple willingness to try something your heart desires. I had always wanted to write for a national women's magazine, so during our evacuation, I called and queried several editors until I got not just one but *three* assignments. Before the flood, I had a hundred reasons not to contact them. But feeling I had nothing to lose, I found that calling editors directly could be enjoyable, not frightening.

When we returned to Grand Forks, I noticed that the people whose lives were improving the fastest weren't the ones doing the riskiest things but rather the ones who seized the change in circumstances to do something they always wanted, such as remodel a room or open a new branch of their business.

Courage isn't supposed to be fearful; it's supposed to be *fun*. It's that I-can't-believe-I'm-doing-this, but-I-am! feeling we get when we're doing something we always wanted to but thought we couldn't. It's what we use after our gift of Dreams has shown us what we'd love to have. The gift of Courage is the first step in transforming a wish into reality.

Ironically, most of us are afraid to have fun. At one workshop, I asked participants to write down one simple thing they'd be willing to do that would be fun for them. The auditorium went silent. People thought and thought, but not one person picked up a pencil. One woman called out, "This is really hard!"

"If I asked you to make a list of ten things you have to do before going to bed tonight, how many of you could do that?" I wondered.

Every hand in the audience went up.

"But you can't think of even one thing that would be fun for you?" I asked.

Another voice called, "We're out of practice!"

So I called a break. As the group was sipping coffee and nibbling muffins, I walked around, listening.

"I'd really love to find someone to go to the community theater with me," one woman said.

"Oh, me, too!" her companion replied. "I just won't make the time to do it otherwise."

"Done!" I said, interrupting their conversation. "You just found the way to use your gift."

I heard another woman say she would love to start a Bible camp. Another person wanted to travel. When we went back into the auditorium, I announced these desires from the stage. Within seconds the audience was abuzz. A woman raised her hand. "You mean we can do what we like?"

You Have the Control

In the old definition of courage, we confront or overcome something we believe is bigger and stronger than we are. We seize control of our lives by taking it back from what appears to have stolen it from us. In the old paradigm, courage is a struggle, a fight, something difficult. The beauty of that is that, inevitably, right and good win out in some way.

With the gift of Courage, something doesn't have to be terribly wrong for you to make it wonderfully right. You begin at a higher place and go higher still, and from that pinnacle, others are inspired to do the same for themselves. When you use your gift of Courage, you'll see that you never lost control to some outside force. Like Dorothy and the ruby slippers in the movie *The Wizard of Oz*, you always had the power to get what you wanted, when you wanted it. But instead of worrying that you have to fight to prove your courage, you simply have to be brave enough to relax and have fun.

This is much, much harder to do than people think, especially for most women. It's been called the Cinderella complex, as in: "If I wash the dishes and clean the floors and do the mending and clean out the ashes from the fireplace and take the kids to school and fix dinner . . . *then* I can go to the ball, but only if my fairy godmother turns up with a great dress and some really hot-diggity transportation." We grow up thinking that it's good to put ourselves last, but in truth, nothing makes us more useless to others than feeling empty, frustrated, or resentful. It takes real courage to say "I'm going to make a priority of doing something that I would enjoy" and following through on that intention. But as you can see from the example above, what you enjoy doing often benefits at least one other person. In other words, when you do what feels right and share the activity with someone else, it's almost impossible for that person not to be set free from his or her own limitations in the process.

Further, it takes courage to have fun because you don't always know what the outcome will be. Unlike a business where goals are set, taking action on your instinct to feel good doesn't always have a clear ending. For most people, this uncertainty is enough to keep them "safe" within the walls of misery and discontent. Adults want to know how things will end before beginning anything new. But all you have to do is look at children under the age of five at play. They usually make up the game—and the rules—as they go about their happy business. And when they're done, you'll rarely hear one say "Gee, I wish I hadn't done that." They discover the joys of life simply by having fun with it.

As you'll see in the upcoming true stories, when you have

fun, the world around you brightens up a bit. By your willingness to take the first step toward what feels right, you will soon discover that whatever appeared to be holding you back was never anything more than a mirage.

MAKING GOOD THINGS HAPPEN

Rather than using your gift of Courage to avoid or overcome something you really *don't* want, you access it by taking the first step toward making something you really *do* want to have happen. All you need to do is ask yourself "What am I willing to try?" Note that I didn't say "What goal do I want to reach?" because for most people, goals are intimidating. As soon as we set them, our predominantly negative thoughts kick in with "You'll *never* reach that!" Or "You *don't* want to work that hard!" Or that "second driver" kicks in with "Wouldn't you rather take a nap than make that call?"

Remember that human beings are motivated by two things: the avoidance of pain and the pursuit of pleasure. With the gift of Courage, you add delight to your life. Having fun delivers us to life in rich, new ways; wallowing in misery makes us fearful and defensive of it. Think of the first time you rode your bike without training wheels, or the day you deposited your first paycheck in the bank. You were doing something new, or perhaps something old, but in a new way. Although you may have been filled with nervous excitement, it still felt good. You were bigger, better, freer than before. No matter what definition of courage you use, that's the result. You find yourself thinking "I can do this!" and feeling *great*.

To find your gift of Courage, start thinking not about the thing that you have never been able to do but the thing you've always *wanted* to do. Then be willing to try it. Simply allow yourself to take the first itty-bitty step toward what would make you happy.

If you need inspiration, observe young children playing. If you leave them alone, you'll see that their imaginations allow them to be anything they want to be, and they have no problem pretending they already have what they want. When my daughters were little, I often complained about having to cook dinner night after night. So they remedied the problem by creating "A and E's Great Restaurant." They set the dining room table with our best china, created a maître d' stand by our front door, and turned on the stereo for some background music. They laid menus carefully on the table and proudly escorted my husband and me to our places. (I lit the candles, however, since they weren't allowed to play with matches.) Then they served the meal: a sumptuous spread of marshmallows, potato chips, and spaghetti with butter. When the bill came, we were allowed to pay it in hugs and kisses. Although the nutritional value of the meal was questionable, the satisfaction we all took from it was not. I tried to get a little more inventive with my own cooking, and the girls continued to do little things that made the serving fun. It was a good solution for all.

For adults, the gift of Courage is a matter of trying to do or invent something that will make things better, easier, or more fun. Although the gift always starts with one person, it's inevitable that when it is put into motion, others will benefit. Here's how one couple used their gifts.

SCOTT AND LINDA'S STORY

Linda was Christmas shopping. She rushed about the streets of Thief River Falls, Minnesota, trying to avoid the 33-degree-below-zero temperatures as much as she could. But as she and her daughters ducked in and out of stores, she noticed that a lost springer spaniel pup followed them every-where they went. He seemed like a happy-go-lucky little puppy, although he was shivering from the cold.

He had no collar or tags, and no owner or master seemed to be about, so Linda and her daughters took him home. They advertised for his owners, but no one responded. They named the pup Patrick, and he quickly became part of the family.

"He was the silliest dog. I fell in love with him fast," Linda says. "He always had a twinkle in his eye. When my daughter was invited to prom, her date came over to see the color of her dress, so he could get a corsage to match. While she was showing it to him, Patrick ran upstairs and got a pair of her purple underpants and brought them down. She wasn't too happy, but we all laughed."

Patrick became a regular at Thief River Linen, the bedding and home furnishings manufacturing company owned by Linda and her husband, Scott. "He never missed a day of work," Linda says fondly. "His job was to boost staff morale and mooch treats."

Patrick lived to the ripe age of sixteen and died in the arms of his human family. But Linda was devastated. "For months afterward, I just couldn't let him go," she says.

On a buying trip to London, Linda passed by a humane society, and realized that Thief River Falls and Pennington County did not have one. She also realized that Patrick was one of the "lucky few," as strays in Pennington County were first impounded and later killed if their owners were not found. She decided that Patrick's memorial for his "brothers and sisters of the street" would be the creation of a shelter that might help other strays connect with a human family.

It wasn't long before the Pennington County Humane Society was born. But there was a problem: How to fund it continually? "The question is always 'How do you raise the money?'" Scott says. "You can look for people to contribute or do an endless number of raffles and sales. But many of those efforts gather in only a little bit of money, and you have to keep going on and on doing them."

Instead, Linda and Scott used their gift of Courage to try something fun. They created the "Patrick of Pennington" line, which made its debut at the national furniture markets in High Point, North Carolina, in October 1998.

"We developed pet-theme products by Thief River Linen which would have inherent value and appeal," Scott says. "Most pet products are cute or sentimental. Ours are in keeping with our overall product line—more high end. A portion of the profits provides a continual stream of revenue to the Pennington County Humane Society."

Linda and Scott went to market with four animal-theme pillows that their daughter had designed and a pawprint tote bag. They also had a picture of Patrick on their display and gave away a card that told more about him. They were overwhelmed with the response. They came home with more than $3,000 in donations and more orders and offers to help expand the line than they expected.

The Patrick of Pennington line now includes the pillows and tote bags designed and produced by Thief River Linen; a pawprint umbrella designed by Raymond Waites; lamps produced by Tyndale; and a dog bed by Old Biscayne with dog linens by Thief River Linen. Linda and Scott's niece is designing hand tags for the products with a small dog biscuit included on each one. There is a promise that more will follow.

"We want this to be something that other humane societies around the country can use for fund raisers, too," Scott says. "It feels good to capitalize on our business connections in a charitable way. Plus, since we've had our humane society, we've been able to move more animals into foster homes and permanent placements."

"Patrick was hardly a 'distinguished gentleman,' " Linda

says, "so this is a good reminder of how easy it is to take an action, how we all can bring changes about." Linda says she was delighted with the response from their business colleagues. "Markets are where people are usually into money making," she says. "But the Patrick of Pennington story added a human, tender element that created something so much better than selling.

"I would have never known some people's love of animals if this hadn't happened," Linda continues. "One woman's eyes misted over as I talked to her. And I've seen Scott jump into this more than I thought he would. I love being surprised in a positive way by someone I think I know."

According to Scott, the most significant development has been the creation of the humane society itself. "There have been eight or ten people who have worked furiously to make this happen," he says. "First, they helped improve the situation at the city pound and opened up their homes to provide foster care for the animals. They also recruited other people to open their homes to the animals.

"The effort has been tremendous," Scott continues. "To whatever extent the humane society has been successful—and we have lots of numbers and figures to prove we are—it's the work of these people that have made it possible. The effort of the volunteers has really blown me away. There is now an incredibly dedicated core of people involved in the humane society."

While Linda and Scott were introducing the line, they received a call from the president of the humane society telling them that an old dog who looked a lot like Patrick was in the pound, scheduled to be shot. She asked if they would like to adopt him, instead.

Buddy, an "aging gentleman," according to Linda, now sleeps happily under a soft pink blanket by the side of Linda and Scott's bed and joins them at Thief River Linens every day.

* * *

Linda and Scott showed courage not because they took in a homeless dog or started a humane society or even used their business to try to create a stream of charitable revenue. Their courage was in allowing their love of their dog and all animals to be evident. Just as the gift of Love helps us see beauty in the people around us and the gift of Dreams is the way for us to see it in ourselves, the gift of Courage makes love public. In an age of tabloids and tell-alls, most of us are afraid to show what's inside our hearts, fearful that it could be distorted or used against us. But when we use our gift of Courage to reveal what is right and good about ourselves, we discover that others do not condemn us. Instead, they can't wait to jump on board and align their actions with ours. Linda and Scott put their hearts on the table, so to speak. Because they did, many animals' lives have been saved, and many other people have had the opportunity to express some of their own gifts. Although the gift of Courage is not about risk, when we use it the fear of risk drops away and only the love remains.

Here's how another team used their gifts.

VERA'S STORY

"We had just moved, and I wanted to help my daughter make new friends," Vera says. "By chance, my husband, Chuck, brought home 'Wonder Science,' an eight-page cartoon publication for parents and teachers on scientific principles. It was filled with experiments you could do at home. Even though I don't have a science background, I figured it might be fun for the girls in my daughter's class to try some of the experiments, and I could handle having a bunch of them come over after school. So we sent out a little letter inviting all the girls from her fourth-grade class, and sixteen out of the eighteen showed up!"

That was the birth of "The Brainy Bunch," a group of girls who met weekly in Vera's 230-square-foot kitchen to have fun doing science experiments. There was only one problem: The group quickly outpaced Vera's knowledge of science. "I quickly realized that I didn't have the science background," she says. "So I started recruiting scientists—mostly women, because those were the people I knew." At the time, Vera was director of University Technology Park at the Center for Aerospace Sciences at the University of North Dakota. Her husband was the chair of the Space Studies Department. The group made a space suit, dissected a cow's heart, and studied trees. They sampled "astronaut ice cream" and learned why stomachs rumble.

As word spread about the fun the girls were having, more and more wanted to join. Even with her contacts, it was hard for Vera to keep up with curricular demands of the increasingly popular activity. This was hands-on science, and with all those curious fingers, she knew she needed help. "I'm not a teacher or a scientist—just a parent who loves to see kids ask questions and learn." Fortunately, the wife of one of the faculty members from the Space Studies Department had a new baby and wanted something to do outside of the home. "She had been an educator in a nature center," Vera says, "and agreed to become the curriculum director and main teacher on a volunteer basis."

By the time Vera's daughter was in fifth grade, the Brainy Bunch included more than forty fifth- and sixth-grade girls who met once a week for two hours after school in her kitchen. The group was so large that they were forced to split into two classes. In the third year of the program, when the sixth-grade boys wanted to be part of the action, three sessions were held.

In spite of the work, Vera says she was having endless fun. "I just love kids! I only worked part time, so I could be at the school as the kids were coming out each day. They'd all troop over, we'd eat something like apples and cheese or hotdogs wrapped in croissants, and then we got to do all this fun stuff! I really got to know all those kids."

The Brainy Bunch had ten volunteers and a $500 budget at its outset. By the third year, it had to be moved to a room donated by the park district in the basement of the golf course clubhouse. By then the group had more than fifty volunteers and a $24,000 budget that was "cobbled together from a lot of different sources," according to Mary Beth Kelley-Lowe, a current education specialist with the group.

As the years progressed, Vera and her team of volunteers kept applying for grants, adding programs and staff, and reaching out to more and more students to join in the fun. The Brainy Bunch expanded to include first through sixth graders, and classes for middle-school students were added. A free, live-in summer science camp for rural and minority students was created, and a Children's Water Festival debuted in 1996.

Then in September 1997 the group, which became known as the Dakota Science Center, struck gold. The U.S. Department of Education awarded the program a five-year, $4.5 million grant, one of only nineteen Technology Challenge grants presented nationwide. With it, the center would create a "virtual museum" called "Nature Shift," where highly skilled Internet technologists would design hands-on learning adventure programs for schools, museums, and state parks. Two months later the group made a bold move when they purchased the flood-damaged First Presbyterian Church in downtown Grand Forks to create both permanent offices and a hands-on science museum. Although the group was not allowed to use any of the federal funds to purchase or repair the building, Vera, her board of directors, their twenty-two paid staff, and more than a hundred volunteers raised enough money to purchase the building outright, so it is debt-free. Now they intend to conduct a major capital campaign to raise the millions needed to remodel it into a true science center.

The benefits of Vera and her devoted team using their gift of Courage extend far beyond the classroom. "We've had kids who've tried to commit suicide," she says. "We have two now who are pregnant. And there have been others with psychological problems so severe that they couldn't attend school. We're there for these kids. They can call us, and we know that's important to them.

"Science centers are wide open. There are no boundaries," she concludes. "You can think and talk and explore in ways that you can't in school. There are days when I go to work and I actually say out loud, 'My God, I love my job!' "

PEACE PROGRESS STEP 5

. . . .

Just One Thing

Using your gift of Courage is not a matter of using everything you've got to battle a foe or change the world. It's simply making the choice to allow your love of or for something to be visible through your actions. When you do this, you ultimately inspire others more than if you did something "heroic," since most people do not believe they are brave, strong, or determined. As you can see from the stories in this chapter, taking a first step invites others to do the same, and everyone is uplifted and feels better as a result.

Go back to Chapter 4 on your gift of Dreams and decide what it is you want most. Once you are clear about that, ask yourself this question:

What one fun thing am I willing to try to make this start to happen?

Note that I didn't say "Make a long list of the tasks and projects that need to be completed and get busy." I said to choose *one* thing and make it fun. Whatever you decide to do should take less than five minutes. And it should be fun to do. It can be a phone call to a friend to discuss the idea or logging onto the Internet to find a supportive resource. It can be jotting an outline, reading a map, checking your bank account, or scouting your cupboards for materials. If you find yourself resistant in any way or for any reason, you're probably not clear enough. Again, refer to the ten questions in the gift of Dreams to help you.

The next part is to try. Not accomplish, not guarantee; just *try*. Trying means to have no expectations and no particular goal. Just "Okay. I'll try this, just this once." You're probably thinking "What happens if I fail?" (I always like to ask people who say that, "What happens if you succeed?" Most of us actually are more scared of success than we are of failure.) You should know that there is no failure when you use your gift of Courage. You may not have gotten quite as far as you would have liked, but you're farther along than you were because now you know what doesn't work. My friend Duane says that when things go wrong, he gets down on his knees and says, "Thank you, God, for showing me what I absolutely, positively do *not* want!"

The next thing to note is that your goal in this process is to make something start to happen. Not "happen" or "finish happening": *Start* to happen. Just get the ball rolling. The true beauty of using your gifts is that once you do, all kinds of wonderful "coincidences" appear in your life. Things get easier and less stressful as you begin to realize that the world is basically a playground designed for your enjoyment. Begin something good, and you won't believe how quickly others will want to join in and pour their hearts into it, too.

Once you've made your choice, *just do it*. If you must,

give yourself a reward, such as a candy bar or a night at the movies for doing so, although usually the good feeling you get is reward enough. If you're the kind of person who responds better to negativity, then enlist your family and friends to give you a really hard time until you take your one step. Steve Levinson, whose book was mentioned earlier, tells the story an overweight man who knew the only way he would ever lose weight was to stay out of restaurants, where he did most of his overeating. So he put up posters around his neighborhood that said "$25,000 Reward to Anyone Who Catches This Man Eating in a Restaurant." He kept the money and lost the weight.

Which leads to one last point: Using your gift of Courage isn't supposed to hurt. Doing so is supposed to be *fun*. So if whatever you decide doesn't feel good, don't do it. You should be feeling good and enjoying yourself, which in itself is a gift to those around you.

Have Courage. And have a good time.

. . . .

CHAPTER SIX

The Gift of Unity

THE GIFTS OF Faith, Love, Dreams, and Courage help you rid yourself of what you no longer want and start to attract more of what you do. By now, your stress level should be lower and you should be starting to feel a calmer, more peaceful sense of control over your life. If you do, then you are ready to discover your gift of Unity. Once you begin to use this gift, you'll find that your world is brighter, more abundant and ready to serve you than you thought.

The gift of Unity can be summed up in the question "Who can help me?" During the flood, that question was asked, and answered, many, many times. We human beings are joined heart to heart. You often will hear people say "I feel your pain." And it is remarkable how quickly we will respond to try to alleviate it.

Before we all evacuated, calls went out from neighborhood to neighborhood for sandbaggers as the dikes developed cracks. Often within minutes, people arrived by the dozens. Before dawn on April 18, the evacuation sirens sounded in our neighborhood. But Steve discovered a huge crack in the dike across the street from our house and wanted to shore it up before we left. I called friends on what was then the dry side of town to come and help; some, leaving their cars at home, walked miles through backyards to avoid the National Guard checkpoints to try to get to us.

But even with the extra hands, we were losing the battle. We called for backup but were constantly told that none was available because other dikes were also in trouble. All we could do was watch, wait, and hope.

A little after noon, a bus filled with people showed up. Then another, and another. These were followed by a National Guard truck piled high with sandbags. As the sandbag lines formed and the work commenced, I turned to the man next to me. "Where did you all come from?"

"Lincoln Park," he answered. "The dike there just broke. I watched my house go under."

I was dumbfounded. "Why are you here? You shouldn't have to work at this anymore."

He shrugged. "Because maybe I can help save your house."

Within hours we had not only fixed the leak, but we had raised the height of the dike several more feet. And even after the disaster occurred, the Central Park dike was never destroyed, although water inundated the neighborhood from the surrounding flooded areas.

UNITY IS NOT DEPENDENCY

While the gift of Unity can be used to tame trouble, it's more fun to use it to launch a dream or expand on the fun created by our courage. The challenge to using our gift of Unity this way is that most of us don't like to admit we need or want help. So it is important to note that when you are using your gift of Unity, you are *not* being dependent. The only way to use this gift is to be involved yourself, contributing as much, if not more, than the others who are using their gift with you. Dependency makes you smaller in relation to someone else; when you use your gift of Unity, you are made larger, and so is everyone else involved.

And there is one more challenge to using our gift of Unity. When you use it, there can be no "buts." In other words, you cannot choose to use it and then say "Sure, I want others involved in helping me manifest my dream, but only if they do it my way." The gift of Unity promises that we are of one heart but not necessarily of one mind. When you use this gift, you have to do so knowing that whatever you set out to do will likely end up differently than you first imagined it would. If you're feeling the need to try to control everything that happens, you are not using your gift. Try using your gifts of Faith and Love until whatever it is you fear falls away.

In every case I've seen, where there is no resistance to the energy and ideas that others bring to the effort, things have turned out delightfully well for everyone. The key is to view others as adding to the success of whatever it is you're trying to do, not see them as making your life more complicated. Unity is a very powerful gift because it includes the first four: Faith (all possibilities), Love (the beauty and good in others), Dreams (clarity about what is wanted), and Courage (the willingness to have fun).

Think of the gift of Unity as your spiritual tool to help you create something pleasurable that would be impossible for you to do alone. Here are the stories of some people who did that.

THE JORDANS' STORY

All of Marge and Carmen Jordan's children can tell stories of the sacrifices their parents made on their behalf. "I remember walking to Christmas Eve mass with my father," Suzi, the eldest, says. "I had on brand-new leather shoes, the color of mahogany. They made a wonderful crunching sound in the snow. And when I looked over, I noticed that my father had holes in his shoes, with plastic bags stuffed in the toes."

"When there were just ten of us, Ma used to pack a picnic lunch, our towels and swimsuits, and we'd pile onto the bus to go down Lake Shore Drive and spend a day on the beach," Janey remembers. "But she'd still be home in time to get supper on the table for Dad when he came home from work."

"Ma's always been there for me," Davy says. "When my first business failed, she helped me find the courage to try again. 'You'll get it all back, and more,' she said."

"My parents always said 'Anything good is what you work hard for,' " Joe says. "When my father wasn't walking a beat as a policeman, he was pumping gas or selling Christmas trees. My mother would often take care of all of us all day and then go out to work at night."

So as Marge and Carmen's wedding anniversary approached, their children wanted to do something special for them as a gift. "You go visit relatives," the children suggested. "We'll scrape and sand the outside of the house and get a professional painter to finish it as our gift to you." The couple agreed, and the eight of their fourteen children who lived in the area, plus their spouses and children, went to work.

Although the Jordan crew had five days to do the job, with everyone working together, it took less than one. As the painter worked, the family talked. They decided that the old porch looked shabby next to the new paint job and that the best thing to do was replace it. "And Ma's always wanted a deck out back," Davy said. "Who wants to help?"

Again, the work got done in record time. With the porch in shape, the two old front doors looked terrible by comparison, so the family replaced them, too. That decision led to the one to replace the vinyl floor and wallpaper in the front foyer of the ninety-year-old house, which resulted in the choice to rewallpaper and refixture the main-floor bathroom. With seventy-two hours left before Marge and Carmen came home, the children and grandchildren met.

"What d'ya say?" Suzi, the eldest, asked her siblings, children, nieces and nephews. "We could finish remodeling the entire downstairs before they get home if we go 'round the clock."

"You can have my strong back," Joe said. "Between my two jobs and this, I probably won't get any sleep, but it's worth it."

"We'll need materials," Davy said. "We can charge it to my account at the lumberyard. I'll get it paid off somehow." He smiled. "I love spoiling Ma."

"I can clean late at night, after Ray gets home to stay with the kids," Jayne said.

"I can stencil the dining room walls and make new curtains," May volunteered. Even Annie, the youngest of the siblings and who was mentally handicapped, wanted to help. "You can be the official wallpaper-smoother and nail picker-upper," Suzi said.

And so, Davy, Suzi, Joe, Jayne, May, Maggie, Liz, Annie, Stan, Joyce, Ray, Ski, Jessey, Jennie and Rusty got back to work. As Davy worked on the deck, Stan was rebuilding the flower boxes for Marge's day lilies and impatiens. Suzi tore out the ancient cabbage-rose linoleum floor from the kitchen. Ray started making plans to replace the roof later that month. Jennie ran for soda pop.

They recarpeted and repainted the living room. They installed a new floor, wallpaper, and curtains in the dining room. They replaced the floor and restored the original tin ceiling in the kitchen. Suzi bartered for new kitchen cabinets, and Maggie and May took on the payments for a new stove, washer, and dryer. The other siblings brought or bought meals to feed the crew. By the last day, even the pizza delivery boy was on his hands and knees, helping in the dining room.

The last nail was driven just as Marge and Carmen pulled into the driveway. "The house looks nice," Marge said as she admired the paint job. Then she noticed the deck out in back. "Oh! And a deck! Just what I always wanted!"

Her first step on the porch brought more surprises. "The porch, too? You kids sure have been busy . . ."

And as she and Carmen set foot in the house, tears began to flow. "Oh, for crying out loud . . ." was all she could say as her children hugged her. Carmen, never at a loss for words, was totally speechless. It took the couple forty-five minutes to go from their front door to the back door in the kitchen, marveling at each project along the way.

"Every one of our kids is special," Marge says as Carmen nods in agreement. Together, using their gift of Unity, they built a beautiful home and a lot of happy memories of the effort.

People often mistakenly think they can use their gift of Unity only with those they know. They're willing to call a close friend or perhaps a family member, either because they feel there's less chance of rejection or because they just don't know where else to turn. In the case of the Jordan family, working together was a natural, familiar thing. Suzi said that their family plans often mushroom, although the house remodeling was by far the biggest project they ever attempted. "What was amazing was how well we all got along," she adds. That's Unity.

But what happens if you're a stranger in a community? Even if you're not, what if your immediate circle of friends and/or family can't help you? Here's what one woman discovered.

JANE'S STORY

"I can't do this alone," my friend Jane said when she called. "I want to help Vera get her book in print, but there's no time to go through traditional publishing channels. She might not live that long."

Vera was a member of our writers' group. She had come to America from Czechoslovakia and wanted to tell her story of what it was like to be a child under Hitler's dominance during World War II. Although she was not Jewish, her story was compelling and clearly showed the horrors of war through a child's eyes. She also pointed out that little had been written about the oppression the Czechs suffered under Hitler, and she wanted to speak out for her former countrymen. She was writing the book for middle-grade readers, fourth through sixth grades, in the hope that the next generation would be more sensitive and proactive in preventing war.

Unfortunately, Vera developed ovarian cancer while she was writing her book, and her future was, at best, uncertain. Jane, the most published author in our group, knew the book business well. "If we want to see this in print, we'll need to self-publish it," she said.

"What's involved?" I asked, knowing she had plenty of experience watching her own books go from manuscript to bookstore shelves.

"We'll need typesetters. I can help Vera with her writing style, but we'll have to have at least one good editor with a keen eye for grammar. We'll need a graphic artist to do the cover and layout, proofreaders, and a good printer. Then we'll need someone to pay the bill—my guess is that it'll be between three and four thousand dollars. Finally, we'll need to have book signings and author's parties for her. It's a lot to do."

I knew that Jane was writing, teaching, and touring in addition to caring for her husband and three children. "You're right. If you're going to pull this off, you'll need lots of help," I said.

"That's the problem."

Jane's heart was in the right place; it was her schedule that wasn't cooperating. "I think I know how to get everything you need."

"How?"

I smiled on my end of the phone. "Ask."

I offered to send a letter to the Mailbag, the op-ed page of the *Grand Forks Herald* where readers' opinions were printed. Although this wasn't exactly an opinion, it certainly would be of interest to the community. I outlined Vera's situation in the letter and asked for all the things Jane had mentioned. Any English teachers out there? A benefactor or two? Anyone like to throw parties?

I gave the number of the English department at the University of North Dakota, where Jane taught, as the contact point. She had figured on a handful of phone calls. But twenty-four hours later, she called me with another problem.

"My office mates are overwhelmed," she said. "The phone's been ringing off the hook!"

I laughed. "People have good hearts, don't they?"

Just a few months later, Vera's book was in print. It had a cover that was beautifully designed by a professional graphic artist who donated her time, and a section of photographs she laid out inside. Thanks to a volunteer team of typesetters and editors from the university, the story unfolded beautifully, page after page. The printer gave his lowest possible price on the job, and the bill was paid by a businessman who chose to remain anonymous and a flurry of small donations from well-wishers. When the book later earned back its costs, Vera offered to repay her benefactor, but the word came back that she should keep the money and use it for further medical treatment, if necessary. There was not one but several author's parties and a couple of other book signings, as well.

Jane oversaw the entire effort. Although she knew some of the people who helped, many were strangers to her at the outset. But by using her gift of Unity, not only was she able to make her friend's lifetime dream come true, she was able to delight in the fact that Vera's health was buoyed in the process. For among the calls and letters that came in, many arrived just to say "We'll pray for you," or "You have our love and best wishes." Vera was surrounded by well-wishers throughout the entire process, and she looked radiant at her first author's party. She outlived her doctors' prognosis not just by months, but by years.

The gift of Unity is the perfect tool to use when we are clear about what we want. Most people want to be good, to be a valuable part of something. But they don't know where to start or what to do. When someone gets sick, we tell our friends, "Let me know what I can do." I don't know of anyone who will admit that they'd love to have someone come over and do their laundry, chauffeur their kids, or take care of a sick family member so they can get some much-needed rest. In many situations, it's obvious what is needed or what might be helpful. If we question more specifically— "Would it make your life easier if our church group arranged to provide you with dinners for a while?"—we discover that it's not as difficult to make wonderful things happen for others as we might have thought.

Here's the story of one man who acted on the promptings of his heart.

BOB'S* STORY

Leslie* was pregnant. She didn't have an easy time of it, and as the months passed, she used up most of her paid sick leave and vacation time from her job. "Even though I'm allowed to take six weeks off when the baby comes, we can't afford for me to have four of them be unpaid," she told Bob, her coworker. "So I guess I'll just take the two paid weeks I have remaining and come back to work."

Bob was healthy as a horse. For many years he had hardly ever been sick. He wanted to help Leslie, and eventually he hit on the idea of donating some of his accumulated sick-leave days to her. His employer searched the company's policy manual and talked it over with him. "There's no reason why you can't," they said. "That's a really generous thing for you to do."

The only thing Bob ever bragged about was his golf game, so he simply smiled humbly. "And I was thinking," he said, "would it be okay if some of the others wanted to donate some of their sick days, too?"

Again, the request was allowed, with one caveat: "If you ask the rest of the staff, make sure they understand that it's strictly volunteer. If they'd rather not, they shouldn't feel pressured into donating."

Bob nodded, and started talking to the others. Some of the staff gave a full week's worth of sick days. Others gave a single day or a few hours, whatever they felt they could. In all, they created a paid maternity leave of not the usual six weeks but seven.

They gave the receptionist a card signed by the entire group. "Have a happy baby!" they wrote. "Enjoy your time off! Good luck—we'll be thinking of you!" Leslie and her husband expressed their heartfelt thanks in a note that stayed on the company bulletin board for weeks, but ac-

*Names have been changed by request.

cording to Bob, it was their smiles and their beautiful daughter that told the story best. When the gift of Unity is used, a very special kind of peace is born.

PEACE PROGRESS STEP 6

. . . .

Many Hands, One Heart

When you use your gift of Unity, you will discover two things: There are people who will say yes to your request and other people who will say no. Contrary to what you might believe, the people who say no are just as valuable to your effort as the people who say yes. "No" is an honest answer, and someone who chooses not to participate in something would only slow or derail your efforts if you somehow convinced him or her to get involved. When you use your gift of Unity, never, ever try to shame or coerce someone else. There is no peace in that—for you or the other person. Like Courage, Unity includes willingness. Someone who is involved out of guilt or fear will make the ultimate experience less enjoyable for everyone. You want contributors, not complainers.

There is one prerequisite to using your gift of Unity: *vision*. You must know what you hope to accomplish, although as stated earlier, the end result is likely to be bigger and better than you first imagine. If you really want others to climb aboard, you're going to have to give them some idea of where you're headed. You can have a specific destination in mind, as Jane did, or it can be more open-ended, as Bob's idea was. In the Jordans' case, their destination was not fixing the house but rather their parents' surprise and joy.

You do not need to be a master communicator to explain your idea to others. In all three examples used in this chapter, the vision was shared either in one-to-one conversation, in a group brainstorm, or in a simple letter of request. You can certainly create brochures, Web sites, advertisements, and a public platform to make your case, but then you're likely either to be starting a company or running for political office. Be careful not to confuse Unity with consensus. You're not trying to get people to agree with you; you're trying to give them a valuable reason for them to be themselves.

So before you go out looking for others to help you, make sure you feel good about what you're about to do. If you're trying to help someone else, make sure you know that person well enough to be certain that what you're creating will be welcome. If you're trying to help yourself, ask yourself what others have to gain by their involvement.

Then ask. There's no other way to use your gift of Unity. Open your mouth, get on e-mail, write a letter, send a fax. *Ask.* People cannot read your mind, so you must share your idea and give them some kind of picture of what they can do to help. In some cases you'll need to be specific and give instructions. In others you'll simply welcome whoever wishes to contribute and let them decide how they wish to do so. One of the things the Jordans mentioned is that after they did the structural work, they had disagreements over how the house should be decorated. They got past that problem by letting whoever put in the most work on the room decide how that room should look. Although the end result was a little eclectic, Marge and Carmen love it because they say it reflects their children's individuality.

You can ask family, friends, or strangers. These days, with the Internet, it is easy to reach out to the world. I have been involved in several prayer chains for people I have never met, and thousands of strangers have joined me in the ones I set up for others. I have a simple rule for approaching those I have never met: I introduce myself. You can, too.

If you don't know whom to ask or where to start, get quiet and ask God to give you some hints. Then you'll likely see a newspaper headline or hear a song you might otherwise have overlooked. You'll bump into someone you haven't seen in years or get a phone call out of the blue. It's great fun to use your gift of Unity this way, as it will broaden your horizons all the more and make you more certain than ever that you can rest easy, because there really is a force much larger than you in charge of things down here.

And what happens if someone says no? Say "Thanks for considering it," and move on. No hard feelings, no regrets. You're no worse off than you were before you asked that person and now you have a clearer idea of what might interest him or her in the future. Before you go, however, ask if the person knows someone else who might want to participate. Just because someone can't be involved or doesn't have time doesn't mean he or she can't be of service.

One final note: Always follow the path of least resistance when you use your gift of Unity. This gift could also be called "the gift of Amazing Energy" because of what it is able to accomplish. But you will get satisfying, peace-producing results only if you "go with the flow." You're not trying to cut a path with a machete through a dark and dangerous jungle; you're simply doing what you can, *because you can*. And so is everyone else involved. If you find you cannot go in a particular direction, get together and figure out a detour. You'll probably like the scenery better anyway.

Many hands, one heart. It's like conducting a symphony. *"And if music be the food of love, play on. . . ."*

. . . .

CHAPTER SEVEN

The Gift of Joy

IN THE JEWISH tradition, we set out a cup of wine for the prophet Elijah on the holiday of Passover. Elijah is the prophet of peace, God's messenger, and we always hope to see him at our table. In fact, we open the front door for him, even when the holiday comes mid-winter in North Dakota. We fill his cup to the "tippy top," as my kids used to say. The cup is so full that if you lift it, it spills over. I once asked a rabbi why we did this. "Because when it comes to joy, we don't cheat God," he said.

That's because God doesn't cheat us, either. The Creator gave us our gift of Joy so we could *thrive* in life, not merely survive it. More than any other species, we have the capacity to take enormous pleasure from our experiences, both real and imagined. In fact, science has proven that our bodies don't know the difference between something we're actually experiencing and something we're just thinking about. If you doubt this, simply imagine the delightful sight, smell, flavor, and texture of a freshly baked cinnamon roll, warm from the oven, in your mouth. You will start to salivate, even though you are not chewing on a "real" roll. So whether we're in a happy situation or not, God has given us both the biological and the spiritual tools to revel not only in what is happening at the moment but also in what we'd like to see happen in the future.

Unfortunately, few of us do. In my workshop, "If I'm Doing Everything Right, Why Is Everything Going Wrong?" I point out to my participants that most of us resist what makes us happy. We have dozens of reasons for doing so, from the guilt we think we are supposed to feel over abundant delight to the superstitious fear that if things get too good for us, they're bound to turn bad. "It's too good to last," we say, or "No one deserves to be that happy." Somewhere in our evolution, we mistakenly learned to equate joy with selfishness or, worse, with impending disaster.

"BUTTING" OURSELVES OUT OF HAPPINESS

I also like to point out to people that we habitually "but" ourselves out of happiness. We qualify everything, limiting our joy. For example, ask someone how their holidays were and they'll likely answer, "Oh, Christmas was great, *but* I gained ten pounds." If they talk about their children, you'll hear something like "Johnny got straight As last semester, *but* he didn't make the football team." Compliment them on a job well done, and you get, "Thanks a lot, *but* I didn't get that last piece of the project the way I wanted it to be."

With the gift of Joy, we are granted permission to turn those "buts" into "ands." For example, ask how the holidays were and with the gift of Joy you get, "Christmas was great, *and* all my kids were home." Johnny's situation becomes "Johnny got straight As last semester, *and* he tried out for the football team. *And* he did his best, even though he didn't make it." What about the job? "Thanks a lot. I worked hard, *and* I really appreciate your compliment."

The gift of Joy is incredibly easy to find but difficult to use. The reason it's difficult is because to access it, we first have to stop running from or resisting what would enjoy. Simply put: We have to grant ourselves permission to be happy. That opens the door. Many people have difficulty doing this not because they don't want to feel joy but because they feel guilty or have superstitions about it. Some have forgotten how. Or maybe they never knew how in the first place. We are so habituated to feeling limited, disappointed, and worried that it can be a challenge to open up to something better. We have a well-made emotional armor to protect us from trouble, which makes it all the more difficult to let it down long enough to "let our light shine," so to speak.

To use our gift of Joy, however, we must do so. It is impossible to be both happy and unhappy at the same time, and so if you want to use your gift, you'll have to decide to let down your guard. While it's true that all our self-protective rationalizations keep out most major difficulties, they also block anything good from getting in. Like the other gifts, Joy is a choice. It's a bold one, one that will deliver you to a new level of freedom and thus peace.

HAPPINESS CAN BE PART OF EVERY DAY

Because most of us believe that happiness is fleeting, we think God's gift of Joy is a hit-or-miss experience. But it's not. We have the power to use it in any given moment and in every single day. We don't have to live without it for a minute, much less a lifetime. Joy is synonymous with the will to live. It's the hope we have that today will be better than yesterday, and tomorrow better than today. It's what people regret on their deathbeds—that they haven't *lived* enough. Translation: They haven't had enough joy. Allow it, and it will make every action more meaningful, every interaction more satisfying, every possession more fulfilling.

When we don't use our gift of Joy, we are merely busy, shuttling from here to there and getting things crossed off our "to do" lists but never feeling a sense of satisfaction. How many times has your spouse asked you what you did all day, and you answered, "Nothing"? Through the years, I have watched countless colleagues in my offices struggle to finish long lists of tasks and, as they do, they either delete them from their computers or cross them off on a paper list. So what do they have at the end of the day? Nothing! (If you're curious, I give myself a star with a bright red pen when I finish a task.) With our gift of Joy, we munch away on life, discovering to our great delight that no matter how delicious this moment is, there's always another that's even tastier waiting for us just ahead.

Most of us can clearly identify at least one thing we think would make us happy, something we assume we lack. "If I only had _____ ," we say, "*then* I would be happy." But when we use our gift of Joy, we take our pleasure from what is right here, right now, knowing that wherever we are, whatever we're doing, and whoever we're with is what we have created with our other gifts. Where there is joy, there is no lack and no regrets.

We stifle our joy for the same reasons we struggle with out gift of Faith. We are in the habit of thinking that we aren't getting what we want, that whatever we're doing isn't going right, and that we can't have what we truly want. More than 80 percent of the time, we are saying "No, no, no!" to joy. Or, more accurately, we're saying "Yes, but . . ." which limits the gift.

We don't have to scream "Yes, yes, yes!" in order to use this gift; we just have to stop resisting, stop saying no. Instead of thinking "This isn't what I want, and neither is this, or this," we merely need to focus on what is okay. You could be contrary and say, "What is *not* wrong?" Or, more productively, "What is going *right* here?" As long as our attention is on responding to what feels good and right to us, we are using our gift of Joy, and more will be added. Each moment becomes money in our bank of personal happiness.

JOY IS A DEEP KNOWING THAT ALL IS WELL

The gift of Joy is not mere exuberance or excitement, however. It is not just a burst of emotion that erupts when everything is perfect. Instead, it starts with a sure and steady knowing that all is well in that moment. When we use our gift of Joy, we have absolute, unshakable certainty that we are expressing the best part of ourselves, the part that makes us, and our corner of the world, a little brighter, bigger, bolder. This is because our gift of Joy does not ask "What would make me happy?" Rather, it helps us answer the question "How can I best share or express my happiness?"

COMING HOME TO JOY

I discovered the gift of Joy when we returned home after our six-week evacuation. Even though we had lived in our house for almost sixteen years by that time, it felt foreign to me. Our garage had to be emptied of flood-soaked possessions, and so did our basement, leaving both eerily bare. The whole house had a damp, musty odor that lingered for months, even after we had the basement professionally sanitized, shivered through cold spring nights with open windows, and bought an expensive air cleaner. As the house resettled, the old plaster walls and even some of the newer sheetrocked ones cracked. All around us, houses were condemned with bright yellow tape or pink signs that warned residents and visitors to be careful or not to enter at all. We were in our own house, but it hardly felt like home.

I was constantly burdened with thoughts of what I

hadn't gotten done or what wasn't the same as before. The harder I worked to make things right, the more things felt wrong. I knew I had to take my attention away from what was bothering me in order to make it fade, but first I had to figure out what I wanted to pay attention to instead.

That wasn't easy. I was surrounded by damage and debris everywhere I looked. People were hauling out mountains of flood-ruined belongings to the curb for the sanitation workers to collect, a process aptly named "mucking out." Toby Baker, a local radio station personality, pointed out that a phenomenon known as "berm envy" had developed as residents sought to have the biggest and most disgusting pile of trash in their yards. (A "berm" is the land between a homeowner's sidewalk and the street. In North Dakota, this space is quite large, as we pile mountains of snow on them when the streets are cleared during the winter.) It was as if everyone were announcing "My misery and loss is bigger than yours."

Then, right around the first of June, my gift of Joy surfaced. Right outside my home office window were two enormous lilac bushes that dated back to the 1800s. They were almost a full story high and flourished annually in spite of our region's subzero temperatures and fierce winds. One day I looked up from my work, and they were in full bloom. Before my eyes were two glorious clouds of soft purple, resplendent with thousands of lilac cones. I unlocked the double-hung window that separated me from them, pulled down the top glass, took a deep breath, and smiled. I closed my eyes, and I could hear a chorus of martins and robins celebrating spring. A cool breeze floated in from the west and kissed my face, leaving a very sweet taste in my heart.

When I opened my eyes, I realized Joy had been with me all along, but I hadn't noticed. I had been so focused on the "death" and despair all around me that I hadn't taken time to realize that what I had been craving was its opposite, *life*. If I had clarified that desire in my mind, I would have been able to see and sense the lilac bushes long before they actually burst into bloom. I would have smelled the moist grass growing and heard the birds singing. As the leaves on the lilac bushes had turned green and buds appeared, I would have delighted in what I was certain lay ahead. I wouldn't have cheated God.

But the gift of Joy, I discovered, was more than simply noticing something pleasant. As I stared and stared, I began to wonder *why* I was so drawn to these flowers. They had bloomed, and I had enjoyed them, for almost sixteen springs. Why did they mean so much to me now?

The sight or smell of beautiful flowers has always had the power to make me feel happy. But this time was different. The lilacs didn't just arouse my senses; they reflected my deeper longing for a new and better life to begin. What I desired was a sign that that could happen, and the lilacs, which in many ways had endured harsher conditions than I had, gave that to me. The appearance of the lilacs reminded me that even in the face of what felt like death, life goes on.

Even more important, the lilacs reminded me that joy comes and goes. No one can predict when a flower will bloom; it happens naturally, when conditions are right and it is ready. And lilacs, like other perennials, fade within a week or so. They are meant to be welcomed, savored, and then released. I had been wondering and worrying if the joys from my past would ever return. But these lilacs weren't last year's blooms; ironically, thanks to the "manure" in the floodwater, they were fresh and new, bigger, brighter, and heartier than the ones from previous years.

Then I knew why the lilacs made me happy. Not simply because they were beautiful and smelled good, but because they were a symbol of what I had always considered the best part of me: the ability to change and grow. Just as beauty can come and go, so, too, would my present circumstances. I wasn't stuck in a never-ending disaster, as I had feared. Instead, my circumstances were changing, and so was I. The lilacs said "Enjoy us now. And when we fade, there will be other flowers in the garden that will bloom." At that moment, I knew everything was fine. There would be time for me to show my colors and other times to rest and let others burst forth. The garden of my life was still growing.

EMBRACING JOY

The gift of Joy is our ability to recognize a good thing when we see it, usually first in our hearts and then later, in real life. It's our capacity to embrace life body and soul and feel it restore or transform us. Other species know how to get what they must to survive, but the gift of Joy is our exclusive ability to notice, accept and respond wholeheartedly to the life around us.

If you show the world only one of your ten gifts, let it be Joy. People often mistakenly think that we have to whip ourselves into a state of crazed excitement in order to experience Joy, but that's not so. Joy is not a "think positive!" feeling. It's an honest, spontaneous expression of what I like to call "passionate peace" that comes from wholeheartedly embracing and responding to life. A good example is when Italian film director Roberto Benigni exuberantly jumped on top of the seats at the 1999 Academy Awards to bound up onstage and receive his Oscar. His joy was totally unbounded, and billions of people around the globe shared his delight. It's important to note, however, that using our gift doesn't mean we have to behave in outrageous ways. Although most viewers took delight in his unrestrained emotion, few would deliberately emulate it. Joy is awakened through response, but that response doesn't have to be extraordinary in order for us to use our gift.

Instead, the result of using our gift of Joy is better defined as a deep, lasting satisfaction that fills us with energy to enjoy life to the fullest. The feeling it gives is, indeed, delicious, because Joy removes our limits and sets us free. With the gift of Joy, we find our capacity to receive love from life. For those who define themselves as "givers," the gift of Joy is a balance, a refilling of our spiritual well. For those who think the world is a dark, dangerous, and unfriendly place, Joy is a relief.

The gift of Joy is not passive, however. Once we have identified the object or situation from which love is flowing to us and understand why this is meaningful, we must respond deeply, fully, with all our hearts. This is the essence of Joy, to welcome and experience life without fear or hesitation. Joy contains within it the feeling of "My cup runneth over" and the knowledge that our cups can never, ever be emptied. And by our example, it is proof to others that theirs can't be emptied, either.

The first five gifts help us to feel safe and give us the "protection" we need to move forward in life. With the gift of Joy, we take the quantum leap into proactively delighting not only in what we have created but what the Creator and others have created for us. The gift of Joy often requires that we use our gift of Courage to choose an action we know would nourish and uplift us and the others around us as well. It does not have to be as extravagant as jumping on the back of a chair and bounding onto a stage. In the case of the lilacs, I went outside with my favorite basket and a pair of scissors and cut a bunch to grace my pink kitchen counter. Steve took some to our store for the staff and our customers to enjoy. And when a neighbor drove up and asked if she could cut a few, I told her to help herself.

It is easy to use our gift of Joy when times are good, everyone is healthy, and there is reason to celebrate. It is more challenging to use when trouble arrives. But that is what Sandi did.

SANDI'S STORY

Sandi is an artist who loved working in her "magical" home studio. With her cat Thomas curled up contentedly on the floor, she would light an aromatherapy candle, put on some soft music, and start to work.

One of her creations was her "child," Ariane, an adorable fair-haired angel with rosy cheeks, peppermint-pink wings, and an aura of glittering stars who graced the bookmarks, notecards, and magnets Sandi loved to make. Those who saw Ariane couldn't help but smile at her, especially since her presence always accompanied Sandi's favorite saying: "Miracles happen to those who believe!"

Sandi responded to the joy in her life by giving away her Ariane creations freely and generously. She tucked them in handmade cards to encourage her friends and family. She sent them to total strangers she heard were sick. She mailed them to talk-show hosts who seemed to be going through a tough time in their lives. Wherever Ariane went people felt better, which seemed to improve whatever life challenge they were facing.

A few years ago, just after she and her husband, John Foundas, were married, Sandi developed breast cancer. At first she wondered, "Why me?" especially since she made a career out of trying to help others feel good. But as her tears began to dry, her concern for others became dominant once again. At that point, the question uppermost on her mind was not "How do I get well?" but "How do I keep spreading joy to those around me in spite of what's happening?"

With a lumpectomy and radiation, Sandi's prognosis was good. "I wasn't worried about myself," she says. "But I was concerned for those around me."

More than simply knowing what brought her joy, Sandi knew why: Her bookmarks brought a smile to her heart and hope to others when they needed it most. So with John's help, she hit on a plan. She hand-colored and laminated more than one hundred of her Ariane bookmarks with the "miracles" saying on them. Then she gave them to him.

"I don't want you sitting in some waiting room worrying while I'm in surgery," she said. "Go spread some hope."

And he did. For several hours, John walked around the hospital, quietly placing his wife's angelic bookmarks where he felt inspired to do so. He left one by a pay phone and tucked another in the phone book that lay on the shelf beneath. He placed them by the coffeemakers in waiting rooms and dropped some on the tops of stacks of well-thumbed magazines. He laid them on windowsills in public hallways and positioned them in Bibles. When he returned to the waiting room for surgical patients, he got a miracle of his own. "Your wife came through beautifully," the doctor told him. "We got it all."

John never looked to see who picked up the bookmarks. But when he left the hospital later that night, he noticed that many of them were gone, swept away, he trusted, by patients, hospital personnel, or visitors who needed a dose of the pure joy Sandi found in giving hope to others.

Today Sandi continues to make bookmarks and magnets. Angel Ariane is just one of her creations. Since her recovery, she has focused on bringing a more earthly life to her work, in the form of petite flowers that she grows, harvests, presses, and applies herself. She spends her days tenderly placing delicate pansy blossoms on cards of parchment stock on which she has written inspiring sayings with her professional calligrapher's hand. For each tiny masterpiece, she picks out two translucent beads, like good makeup to bring out the colors of the flower, tying them on with a vanilla-colored satin ribbon.

Sandi sells her creations to specialty shops and uses them herself to spread joy wherever she goes. "Believe!" "I give you a quiet hour," "When your soul speaks, take good notes," or "You are loved" are just a few of the encouraging things she wishes others. She is legend at local restaurants, where she joyfully responds to good service by leaving a handmade card or bookmark with her tip. She often sends a small garden of bookmarks to people who are ill, even if they are total strangers, hoping they will use her Joy to spread some of their own. She always has a handful of her creations in her purse so she can be ready to hand over some love wherever it is needed.

On the back of each of Sandi's bookmarks and magnets she writes: "Created with a Heart Full of Love." Her joyful cup runneth over, indeed: For every one she sells, she donates a portion of the profits to breast cancer research. Thanks to her joy, thousands—and someday possibly millions—of people feel a lot better.

Joy is contagious. When we use this gift, others are inspired to unwrap their own gift and bring it to light. That's what happened to one man who loved flying.

JOHN'S STORY

John loved flying. He loved it so much that he wanted everyone else to love it as much as he did. When he was young, he flew every chance he got. In fact, he learned to fly aerobatics in a crop-dusting plane, reading a manual strapped to his leg to get the instructions for the maneuvers as he was piloting!

John was never happier than when he was at the controls. With John, every flight was nonstop to joy. He became certified to fly every type of aircraft he could, including jets, single- and twin-engine airplanes, gliders, seaplanes, and more. He loved each one for what it could do and where it could take him, his family, and friends. Weather never stopped him, and neither did distance.

John's favorite poem was by James Gillespie Magee, Jr., a nineteen-year-old aviator who wrote this on the back of an envelope shortly before his plane was shot down during a World War II battle:

High Flight

Oh, I have slipped the surly bonds of earth
And danced the skies on laughter-silvered wings;
Sunward I've climbed, and joined the tumbling mirth
Of sun-split clouds . . . and done a hundred things
You have not dreamed of . . .
Wheeled and soared and swung
High in the sunlit silence.
Hov'ring there,
I've chased the shouting wind along, and flung
My eager craft through footless halls of air.
Up, up the long, delirious burning blue
I've topped the windswept heights with easy grace
Where never lark, or even eagle flew.
And, while with silent, lifting mind I've trod
The high untrespassed sanctity of space
Put out my hand, and touched the face of God.

John flew all during college and revived his school's flying club by getting the necessary support to lease an aircraft and offer flight lessons to students. After he received his undergraduate degree in business and his postgraduate degree in accounting, he was appointed to the faculty of his school. Within two years he had started a department of aviation.

He talked the administration into giving him an office— "It was a converted closet, really," he said—and joined forces with an accounting professor and an aviation entrepreneur to begin organizing some classes.

At first, they had only two things: a clear mission state-ment—"to provide the highest-quality aerospace education at the lowest possible cost"—and John's gift of Joy. John didn't know how they were going to deliver that education, since the new school had no money and, more to the point, no airplanes. But he didn't worry about it—he just kept thinking about how good it felt to fly and how good the students would feel when they learned, too.

A few weeks later, the accountant on the team was meeting with a client, a senior citizen who, surprisingly, had just come into a cash windfall in a business deal. "You really should invest that," the accountant suggested, "preferably by purchasing something big for the university, like two airplanes." The potential donor was reluctant until John offered to give him flying lessons. John was so enthusiastic that even though the man was in his mid-seventies, he wrote the check. Before the month was out, the newly organized aviation department had the beginnings of a small fleet.

Those who worked with John never ceased to be amazed at how his Joy opened doors. "He presented things that sounded totally impossible," says one staffer, "and as we would all shake our heads and talk about why it couldn't work, he kept insisting it would. And you know what? It always did. Sometimes it took several weeks, months, or even years, but eventually, everything he ever envisioned came to pass."

Today, some thirty years later, John's "Department of Aviation" has grown into one of the nation's most widely respected and awarded aerospace colleges. Its enrollment soared from an initial twelve students to more than 1,500 from every state in the United States and many foreign countries. The students now log more than 80,000 flight hours annually in eighty-seven aircraft and fourteen flight simulators. The faculty now numbers more than 500 includes experts not only in flight training but in meteorology, space studies, computer science, and satellite broadcasting, so that classes can be taught to remote students all over the world.

In 1998 the University of North Dakota did something

unprecedented in its history: It named one of its colleges not for a major donor but for its founder. John's Joy, which had become the Center for Aerospace Sciences, is now the John D. Odegard School of Aerospace Sciences. At the naming ceremony, the president of the university said, "Some people give a lot of money to have a college named after them. John gave his life." And, as everyone present knew, his Joy. With ties to NASA and major airlines, John's graduates command not only the sky but outer space, as well.

Sadly, John succumbed to cancer in 1998. But using his gift of Joy, he launched a legacy that has allowed thousands of others to experience the delights of flight both now and for generations to come.

PEACE PROGRESS STEP 7

. . . .

Journaling Joy

I have been journaling, and teaching journaling, for as long as I can remember. For me, and perhaps for you, there is no better way to clarify and state what truly has meaning. This is why I heartily recommend it as a tool to discover and use your gift of Joy.

Journaling is not essay writing, unless you want it to be. It is merely meant to be a record of your thoughts and feelings, identifiable only to you. People always tell me that they worry about others finding their journals. I tell them they shouldn't care, because what you jot or create should be meaningless to anybody but you. You're not writing the Great American Novel; you're getting in touch with yourself. If you want to write for other people, get a publisher. If you want to unleash your Joy, keep a journal.

And while journals are comfortable places to dump all your psychological trash, I no longer use mine that way. A journal that is used only to whine, moan, and complain will merely clarify all the reasons you have to be unhappy. Do that daily, and I guarantee that you will only attract more misery to your life. Instead, think of your journal as your own personal bible. (Note: I mean no disrespect to those of you who use either the Torah or the New Testament as your Godly books. In your case, think of your journal as a celebration of what you learn in those texts.) It's what will draw you closer to our Creator and to all of God's life in this life.

So start by thinking of your journal as a happy, healthy place for you to spend a few minutes each day. Note that I did not say "Set aside an hour a day to journal," because I know most of you won't do that, either because you don't want to or you truly do not have time. Journal when the mood hits you, and spend as much time doing it as you can comfortably and easily. For some of you, that may mean jotting no more than a single word each day, perhaps something that sums up your mood or something you just experienced. I once had a workshop participant write "Darn! Darn! Darn!" as her journal entry for the day. Another merely wrote the word "YES!!!" in bright red pen. As I said earlier, don't worry about anyone else understanding it. When you see what you've written, your memories will be triggered, and you will know what you meant.

You will need a form of a journal that feels comfortable to you. I have several, actually: a file in my beloved computer, a pocket-size book that sits on my nightstand, several large spiral-bound notebooks I use when I travel, and a "pocket briefcase" filled with three-by-five cards that my husband bought me as a gift. I use all of them interchangeably, usually a matter of convenience. No, I don't worry that none of them has an exact chronology; that is not important to me. If it is to you, you will likely want to stick with one type of journal, perhaps a notebook, a series of spiral-bound books, or a computer file you can update daily. Once you've picked the form, get yourself a good pen or a decent monitor and keyboard. You'll want to make journaling as comfortable as possible.

Using your gift of Joy is as easy as 1, 2, 3. Jot these questions in your journal:

1. What is going right (or "What is *not* wrong?") in this moment?

2. Why does this make me happy?

3. How can I best respond to it?

One note: When you get to question 2, stay with it for a while. Try to go beyond the obvious, superficial things by asking repeatedly, like a child, "But why? But why? But why?" It make take days, months, or even years, but sooner or later, you will get to the heart of what you love and achieve new levels of certainty that lead to true and lasting satisfaction.

There are dozens of different ways for you to answer these questions daily without getting bogged down in long treatises. Here are a few things you could try, not only so you don't get bored but to trigger different responses within you.

1. Try jotting one word to sum up your response to any of the three questions. You can either search for this word, or close your eyes and see what rises to the surface.

2. Keep your entry to three sentences or phrases: 1, 2, 3. Bing, bing, bing. Set an egg timer so you do it in three minutes or less. Again, what you're doing is overriding your internal critic, which allows Joy.

3. Clip a picture or a headline from a newspaper or magazine and paste it in your journal as your response to the questions. Study the pictures, and then ask yourself, "Why does this appeal to me?"

4. Use your journal as a scrapbook. When you feel happy, take a souvenir from the moment and paste it in your book. See which question your souvenir answers.

5. Get a camera and take a picture of whatever you notice when you ask the questions. Again, over time, you will see a pattern developing, which will suggest what brings you lasting joy.

6. Use a tape recorder instead of any form of written journal. Oral histories are a great way to journal. Talk out your answers, but again, try to be brief, or you'll never go back and listen to learn more.

7. Write descriptions of how others around you seem to be using their gift of Joy. A good way to learn is to pay attention to how other people do—and do not—use their gifts. Put stars by the ideas that you want to try for yourself.

8. Forget the questions and count your blessings instead. One of the simplest best-sellers of all time is *14,000 Things to Be Happy About* by Barbara Ann Kipfer. It's nothing more than a really, really, really long list of things she noticed that brought a smile to her face. As you read it, you can't help but smile, too. Start a list of things you love in your life, and keep it going for the rest of your life. You'll soon discover what brings out your Joy and why.

9. Pay attention to when you feel tense or unhappy, and quickly jot a note about what you would want instead of what you are experiencing. (Remember: no complaining in your journal. Just write down what you want, not what you don't.) Eventually you will see a pattern, which will lead you to your Joy.

10. Be a kid again. Buy crayons, markers, stampers, or fingerpaints, and play in your book. Give yourself a gold star—or a thousand of them, for that matter—when you're done. Set your intention before you play: to think of what makes you happy and why. Your subconscious will answer, and you will end up not only with a delightfully colored book, but you will be a step closer toward your ultimate peace.

11. Doodle. It's similar to step 10, but with a pen or pencil. In other words, answer the questions graphically or symbolically. For those of you who are visual rather than verbal, it's the only way to go.

12. If you're aural by nature, jot down sounds that seem to respond to the questions. Or, for that matter, scents. Then ask yourself, "What does this remind me of?" Again, that path will lead you to your Joy, and soon you'll be able to discover why and how best to respond.

13. Date the pages, and allow yourself to leave some blank. That's right: Put nothing on them, if that's what you're feeling. You'll quickly discover that a day without Joy feels almost unlived, and you'll be eager to put something—anything—on that page.

14. If you're a computer buff, write an e-mail to yourself every day, answering the questions. Oh, come on—

we all know you're spending hours doing it with total strangers. Talk to yourself. Find your Joy.

And when you do, celebrate! Give yourself some kind
of reward to coming to some sort of conclusion. Remember,
too, that your Joy will change day by day, throughout your
life. So even though you know what makes you happy and
why today, be prepared for it to change—make that *improve*—throughout your life. Notice when you are feeling
happy, and then find a way to respond to what you have
created. As my daughter Erica says, "Ahhh! Life is good!"

CHAPTER EIGHT

The Gift of Trust

WHEN I WAS growing up, one of my favorite Sunday school stories was about God playing a game of hide and seek. He had just finished creating the world and asked the animals, "Where shall I hide so that people will try to find me?"

The bear answered first. "Come into the cave, where I hibernate. They'll never find you there."

God considered this, but then said no. "Sooner or later, they'll find the cave and then they won't look any more."

So the eagle offered a suggestion. "Fly high with me, far, far away from here. They will never be able to travel far enough to find you."

Again, God said no. "Sooner or later, they'll find a way to fly, and they'll be able to cross Earth and then they won't look for me any more."

The highest star spoke next. "Then come into outer space. There are so many stars and they are so far away, they will surely give up before they find or reach you."

"I don't want them to give up," God said. "I just want them to want to search for me. That way, they'll never stop looking for what is loving or good all the days of their lives. And besides, someday they'll be able to reach the stars."

The fish swam over next. "Come to the bottom of the ocean," they said. "It is so dark and deep and there are so many tides and currents that they will always have to struggle to find you."

"Thanks anyway," God said. "But I don't want it to have to be that difficult for them."

God thought and thought. As he did, he saw Adam and Eve romping around the Garden of Eden, looking for one delight after another. They admired the beautiful flowers and listened to the harmonies of the tropical birds. They closed their eyes and savored all the lush aromas of living, growing things. They tasted all the good foods growing around them. They felt the warmth of the sun on their skin and the soft breeze in their hair.

As God watched, he noticed something else: everything that Adam and Eve enjoyed was found outside of themselves. They had not yet learned their own worth in the scheme of things; they had not yet searched their souls.

"I know!" God said. "I will hide in their hearts. They will never think to look for me there."

TRUST COMES FROM WITHIN

Although many Jewish stories are known as *midrash*, spiritual fiction, I knew this one had to be true because as I grew up, I'd get a little pang in my heart every time I did something wrong. It was as if God had put a tiny radio transmitter in there. It didn't just go off when I got in trouble; sometimes, especially when I wasn't thinking about it, I'd get the idea that I should do something nice for somebody, quiet down and listen, or go ahead and have fun. Most of the time, I knew when God wanted my attention by the way I felt.

But every now and then, someone would say something to me that was just what I needed to hear or know, and I'd know that was God coming up from their hearts, too.

Admittedly, I am not a trusting person by nature. Because I grew up near New York City, I was taught not to make eye contact with strangers. Although I had plenty of friends, I found I got hurt less often if I simply played with them rather than told them my deepest, darkest secrets. Besides, I always felt different, since we were one of very few Jewish families in our neighborhood.

Because I had difficulty trusting others, in spite of what I learned in Sunday school, I also had trouble trusting myself. Even though I had the sense that God—or at least a seed of God—was within me, I still went looking "everywhere but here," as the saying goes. For most of my adult life, I was a "seeker," always looking for something or someone else to give me *the* answer to what would make my life work. I read hundreds of books on spiritually. I learned more than one method of mind control, to better tame my thoughts. I listened to motivational speakers. I learned to meditate. Eventually, I began to sense that I needed a lot less learning and a lot more knowing. And that is when the gift of Trust began to surface.

During the flood, I never worried if God was with me, or everybody else, for that matter. I knew He was. The problem was that most of us—myself included—weren't listening. We were too busy talking to the FEMA guy, finding bottled water, and trying to figure out how we could pump out our basements without collapsing the walls to pay much attention to the still, small voice within.

But even as I worked practically nonstop, I found I could hear God whenever I felt good. It was when I was angry, frustrated, or discontent that my internal radio signal got nothing but static. On the days when I stayed close to what felt right to me, I received new insights about what to do next. These always worked out, and again, as long as I responded to the voice in my head saying "Yes, do that," not only was I okay, but so was my family.

So I started paying more attention to when I was feeling good. Or, as with some of the other gifts, when no negative bells or whistles were going off in my gut. "Good" can be defined many ways, including wildly excited good, grinning good, playful good, or peaceful good. There is also smart good, happy-go-lucky good, and passionate good. Soon I learned that it all had value. By paying close attention to when I felt good, I discovered Trust.

Trust is different from the other gifts in that it is the only one to be experienced over time. Although it may be aroused in this moment, it is awakened over many moments—even a lifetime. Using it consistently gives the peaceful certainty that we do, indeed, have the power to create a little bit of heaven right here on Earth. No matter how good our contribution or world service is by using our first gifts, this is the one that puts us on our path and keeps us there. Use it, and you'll never ask the question, as they do in the movie *Down and Out in Beverly Hills*, "How did I get here?"

WHEN DO YOU FEEL GOOD?

The gift of Trust answers the question "When do I feel good?" Notice it does not say "What am I *doing* to feel good?" because the only way you'll ever experience this gift is by listening to the yearnings of your heart. You find it by first deciding and then taking the time to tune in. It's not unlike switching channels on a portable phone or using the scan button on your car radio. To use this gift, you look for the strongest, clearest invisible signal, and try to lock on it. If you go out of range—in other words, if you start feeling restless, anxious, or uncomfortable—you need to redirect your attention to something that feels right to you to get back in touch with it again. Once you do, the idea is to lengthen the "when" as much as possible. Trust is when you're staying within clear, understandable range of the knowledge that you are God's child, and so is everyone else. You know you're using it when love seems to be flowing in your life.

Now that you've learned to surrender your problems, notice the beauty in others, clarify what would make you happy, take a step toward that, have others help you, and celebrate the sense that you're on the right track, you need a gift that can keep you in this better place for as long as possible. That's Trust.

For those who have trouble getting still long enough to tune in, Trust can be experienced in another way, too: by getting out of the way of those who are using their gift to stay on their own paths. When it comes to peace, you can be a follower just as easily as you can be a leader. So when you encounter someone who seems relaxed and at ease with him- or herself, hang around a little bit. You'll probably feel better just by doing that, since energy is contagious. And after a while, you'll probably lose some of your own discomfort, thus taking down some of the blocks to your using this precious gift.

Anne Frank was right: "People are basically good at heart." That goodness is actually their "God-ness," placed there so they would search, and find, the creator within. When we listen and take heed, we are using our gift of Trust. That's what Gail and Duane did.

GAIL AND DUANE'S STORY

Through her tears, Gail could hardly see the typewriter keys. But she pressed on, knowing that she had to write this letter. Slowly, deliberately, she fashioned each word, wanting each one to be perfect.

To the family of Kim Ji Yun:

*Early last fall we received a picture and informa-
tion on a little girl named Kim Ji Yun. From the minute we saw that picture, we knew there would be a
special place in our hearts and in our home for her.
We were so excited and anxious for her to come to the
U.S. and be our daughter, but at the same time we
thought very much about you, her family. . . .*

Upstairs, the reason for the letter slept peacefully in her
new bed. Four-year-old Kim Ji Yun had just arrived from
Korea that morning and was exhausted from her trip halfway
around the world. Gail and her husband, Duane, had just
adopted the little girl, now a sister to their other adopted
Korean daughter, Dayna. Kim Ji Yun would be called Kelsi,
but they had no way of telling her that. The child spoke no
English. She thought she was coming to America to find her
mother, who, she was told, had come years earlier in search
of a piano for her.

*We wanted to let you know that she arrived safely in
the U.S. We also want to let you know that we love
her as much as any parent can love a child and that
we are committed to raising her in as loving a home
as we can provide. We want you to feel confident that
she will lead the life you wished for her.*

Gail had no idea of the person to whom she was writing.
All she had been told was that Kelsi's biological mother had
died and that her father was forced to put her up for adoption.

*We knew only what the history [from the adoption
agency] told us about you—but yet we felt we knew
you somehow. We felt that you have permitted us to*

*care for this very special little girl and we take this
responsibility very seriously.*

Kelsi had brought a picture book with her, a gift from
her father. In it, there were photographs of her biological
mother, her father, and her brother, a boy just a few years
older than she. The pictures show Kelsi and her brother
smiling and playing together, and it was clear as she showed
them to her new family that she missed him.

Although Kelsi would now have a sister, a loving home,
and a chance for a good education, Gail and Duane knew
there would be a part of her that would remain forever incomplete. They wanted to help her retain her love of her
biological family and Korean culture.

*We want you to know that we would be open to cor-
responding with you on a regular basis. If you see fit,
we would like to hear from you.*

Gail signed and mailed the letter to the Korean orphanage, but without much hope. She had written a similar one
when they had adopted Dayna years before and never heard
a word from any of her biological relatives. She had no idea
if Kelsi's father would respond, or if he did, how he would
feel about "sharing" his daughter with another family halfway across the planet. But less than a month later, they received this letter:

To Kelsi's adoptive parents:
    *The May sky is blue and fresh. . . . When I re-
ceived your letter, I was very happy. One of my neighbors translated your letter, therefore I was able to
understand your letter to every detail. I feel lucky that
Dayna and Kelsi are fortunate enough to have loving
parents that provide them with good education and an
easy life. I feel it in my heart that you two will be*

*good role models for them, and I have the deepest
respect for you. I thank you, once again, for taking
good care of Kelsi and Dayna. Their grandparents and
all their relatives are praying for your long and happy
life.*

He went on to tell them about the circumstances leading
up to his reluctantly putting Kelsi up for adoption. After
Kelsi's mother died, a recession caused her father to be laid
off from the factory where he worked. He struggled to make a
living but found only part-time work. Because boys care for
their families in Asian culture, Kelsi's father kept her brother
with him and took Kelsi to the orphanage. But he did not
abandon his daughter; he visited regularly and brought her
gum and other treats. When Kelsi asked about her mother, he
told his little girl that her mother was in the United States,
searching for a piano so Kelsi could learn music.

Things did not improve, and eventually he knew he had
to let Kelsi go. He expressed three wishes that went into her
adoption file: (1) that she find a new mother, (2) that she
get a good education, and (3) that she learn to play a musical
instrument. Within a few weeks, Gail and Duane had
adopted her.

They were thrilled to get the letter and wrote back again
immediately. Soon a stream of letters poured forth between
the two families, ever increasing in love, trust, and respect.
Kelsi's biological father began sending gifts from the Korean
culture, always including Dayna, whom he came to feel was
part of his family, too. Eventually Kelsi's brother also began
to send letters:

My Dear Only Sister:
*I was glad to receive your letter. It seemed that I
was with you when I read your letter. It helped me
know how you are doing. I heard you were worried
about your occupation in the future. So do I. I want*

to choose an occupation that I can give my help to you and your family.

Let's make an effort to become a wise man for many people who are worried about you and me: our father, our mother, who is looking at us in heaven quietly, and your adoptive parents who always love you.

I want you to know that I love you dearly, too. I dream of the day we can meet each other again.

As the years passed, Gail and Duane's trust grew and grew. "We felt no jealousy or fear about Kelsi loving her biological family more than us," Gail says. "In fact, we feel like we have gained a bigger family for ourselves. We consider Kelsi's father like a brother-in-law, and we have been trying to save enough money for all of us to go to Korea for a reunion."

Although Dayna was always included in the correspondence with Kelsi's biological family, she often wished that one of her relatives had responded to Gail's letter. Finally, when she was a teenager, one did. Her aunt wrote and sent pictures, thanking Gail and Duane and telling Dayna more about her biological family. Although the translation was choppy, it was clear that Dayna had a least one sister—possibly a twin. She was elated.

More than a decade later, the families are fast friends. They have shared their ups and downs through the years, including the sadness of Kelsi and Dayna losing three of their grandfathers in less than twelve months: Gail's father, Kelsi's biological grandfather, and Dayna's biological grandfather. More than ever, the families are determined to meet before more deaths occur. But sadly, the money Gail and Duane had saved for the trip had to be used to pay for a special assessment when the county decided to pave their rural street.

Kelsi will graduate from high school in 2001 and plans

to go on for higher study. She plays several instruments, including the piano, organ, drums, and bells. She also loves to sing. Her parents' dreams—both biological and adoptive—did, indeed, come true. Dayna graduates in 2000, and all three parents, as well as her brother and sister, are thrilled.

But the most thrilling development for the two families is that by entering college, Kelsi's brother gained access to a computer. Now the two write to each other daily, including letters like this one:

> I am happy about your great journey. [Kelsi traveled with her high school choir]. Journey always makes us fresh!!! i took a trip, too. My destination is kang-rung. Kang-rung is famous for a beach resort. But i didn't swim. Because i can't still swim and the beach was not opened. i only saw the night of seashore. i was very fantastic scene. i can't explain about it. Did you see the night of seashore?
>
> Father isn't recover from illness, yet. But he is getting better than past time. "Don't worry about it, Kelsi. Because you make me energetic." Father said.
>
> Sometimes, i think English is so easy. But i get tired from English, another times. i can't tell to you only one word about it. Please check this mail and tell me about wrong expression. This is great help to me.
>
> Oh! Time is late. i must go, now.
> Bye my love kelsi !!!!!!!!!!!!!!!!!!!!!!!!!!!!!!!!!!!!!

Gail and Duane adopted not only two daughters but dozens of relatives thousands of miles away. They know they will meet someday, somehow, and that when they do, it will be joyous for all. They have trust.

* * *

Gail not only trusted the voice in her heart when she wrote that first letter; she trusted in the good that Kelsi's biological father has within himself, too. That trust has paid off in ways she could never have imagined years ago, both for Kelsi and Dayna, as well as all of the adults involved. Although Trust is a passive gift, it often inspires action that can transform a situation or a life. In Gail and Duane's case, their trust transformed many lives.

When we use our gift of Trust, we are arousing the good—make that the voice of God—within us. With our gift of Faith, we are appealing to God outside of our physical selves, but it is not contradictory to respond to God within, since God is everywhere and created us. When we do, often we are inspired to action that is even more extraordinary than that inspired by our gifts of Courage. We go beyond thinking that something would be fun to try and boldly say or do something we ordinarily wouldn't, never doubting for a single second that we are doing exactly the right thing. This can and usually is for the benefit of someone else, since Trust makes it easy to reach out to others.

As I said earlier, I am not, by habit, a trusting person. But over the years, I have been fortunate to gain a few friends close enough to know when I hurt, even when I don't say much about it. That's what happened with Sally.

SALLY'S STORY

My husband, Steve, and Bob had been friends since high school. Bob was Oscar to Steve's Felix in their school production of *The Odd Couple* and although college sent them packing to different places in the country, it was easy to rekindle the friendship when both men found themselves back in Grand Forks, Steve to take over his family's retail clothing business and Bob to be an orthopedic surgeon at the local hospital.

I came with Steve, of course, and Bob brought Sally, the wife he had met in college. The friendship enlarged as our eldest children were born within weeks of one another and the others came close behind. We lived within a few blocks of one another and showed up at all the same school functions for years. We swapped house keys, books, recipes, and tools, growing a strong and lasting trust along the way.

Before long, we found ourselves sharing holiday celebrations. Our favorite was "Chrisannukah," an invention born of necessity. When Sally and Bob moved into their stately Victorian home, it called for nothing less than a ten-foot balsam in the living room for Christmas. But with tiny children, it would take a few extra hands to get it decorated properly. So our family was invited to participate in their annual tree-trimming, which often fell on or near the Jewish holiday of Hanukkah. As our children and husbands were placing the last ornaments and beads on the tree, Sally and I would retreat to the kitchen. She would put the finishing touches on one of her amazing roast legs of lamb while I would go whip up a batch of latkes—the fried potato pancakes associated with Hanukkah. And after dinner, we'd set up our family's menorah and pull out some dreidls (tops) for the children to play.

A few years ago, not long after Chrisannukah, Steve's mother fell ill. She had the flu, my father-in-law said, and was too weak to do much cooking. So I stewed up the best medicine I know—chicken in the pot with lots of vegetables—and Steve took it over. His mother was lying on the couch, visibly weakened. Everyone agreed that if she didn't feel better after eating the dinner, she should see her doctor as soon as possible.

By morning she was hospitalized. The news wasn't good: Her vital organs were shutting down, one after the other. "Call your family," the doctor warned. "We don't think she'll last the day."

Steve's sister, our brother-in-law, and their infant daughter caught the next plane up from Denver. By the time they arrived, my mother-in-law was in the intensive care unit, hooked up to full life support. The only organ left functioning was her heart. Her kidneys, liver, and lungs had all shut down, not only from the flu but also from a severe case of emphysema that had gone undiagnosed to that point.

The doctor gave her Valium to keep her from struggling with her ventilator and fluids to rehydrate her body. "Now we wait" was all he could say.

So day after day, my father-in-law, my husband, our daughters, and Steve's sister and her family waited. We got to know the other families in the ICU lounge well as we all waited and hoped for any glimmer of good news about our loved ones. Every time the door to the unit opened, we would all jump. But there was hardly ever a reason—the changes were subtle and largely meaningless.

We spent the long hours sitting, but it was exhausting, all the same. Every now and then, we'd go down into the hospital's basement cafeteria for something to eat, but nothing tasted very good. Coffee in the lounge kept us awake for long stretches, but eventually, even that stopped jolting our senses.

As the days wore on, my mother-in-law's condition neither improved nor deteriorated. We were numb with a combination of disbelief and grief, wondering what to do next. Time seemed to stand still, at least for Steve and me. We sent our girls to school every day, trying to keep things as normal as possible for them, at least. But our house, normally bursting with activity, felt cold and eerily silent. It was too clean and too empty, even though the kids had been home for hours before Steve and I walked in the door. When we did, there were no good smells emanating from our pink kitchen and no laughter in our halls. We'd drag ourselves upstairs and fall into bed, mentally and spiritually exhausted.

Then one day, after Steve put his key in the lock, we

were greeted by something other than emptiness. The crisp smell of fresh garlic tickled our noses, coupled with what was surely tomatoes and oregano. As we stepped into the kitchen, we could see that the table had been beautifully set and graced as well by a loaf of homemade French bread. Beside it was a note:

Dinner's in the stove and the fridge. Enjoy!
Sal

"Oh, boy, Sally cooked!" Steve exclaimed, racing over to the oven. Besides being a close friend, Sally was one of the best cooks in town. She made everything from scratch, including many of the sauces she used. She had whipped up a batch of veal parmigiana with spaghetti, the fresh bread, a green salad, and a fabulous homemade grasshopper pie for dessert.

The girls joined us at the table, and within minutes, we were all talking and laughing as we enjoyed the feast before us. Although the girls knew that Sally was bringing treats, Steve and I did not. She never called to say "Is there anything I can do?" She sensed—or rather, she just knew— what to do, and she did it. No question, no holding back. That's Trust.

A few days later, my mother-in-law awakened and went on to achieve a full recovery. The doctors called it a miracle, and for the most part, we did, too. The experience introduced me to the wonder of prayer chains, for after she had fallen ill, we learned that several had started around town for her benefit. But it also made me realize how important Trust is, not only in ourselves but of the people around us. I can't say that Sally's meal changed my mother-in-law's outcome, but it definitely transformed our mood and the moment, and gave us the mental and emotional lift we needed when we needed it most.

* * *

The gift of Trust has one final characteristic that's important to note. As we learn to trust ourselves and others, we also learn that we can trust life. We may not always know what we want, especially when trouble strikes. But our gift of Trust assures us that we will always know what we need and, by using our other gifts acquire it. Always.

PEACE PROGRESS STEP 8

. . . .

A Minute of Trust

The main reason so few people hear "the still small voice within" is because they're never still. We are constantly bombarded with stimulation from the moment we awaken to the moment we drift off to sleep at night. When I first started my advertising career, I learned that each of us is exposed to more than 250,000 messages a day! And that was over twenty years ago, before anyone talked about the Internet. (Now experts say it is more like a million messages a day.) They come to us as labels on our tubes of toothpaste, the state slogans and car dealer insignias on the cars around us, the labels on our clothes and more. All this is in addition to whatever we pick up on radio, television, billboards, through the mail, or on the net. The latter probably has doubled the number of information "hits" many of us receive daily, thanks to the banners and "cookies" on most Web sites.

It's easy to develop somewhat of a thick skin to all of this stimulation. Like an infant, there's only so much of it we can take. So we dull our senses and tune out most of the time. This, however, does not make us spiritually aware; just the opposite. When we unconsciously go within, what we hear is the noise in our own brains, which, as stated earlier, has more than 40,000 negative impulses a day. Instead of being soothed by our mental isolation, we are upset by it, causing all kinds of fears and worries.

Because Trust is a key ingredient in personal peace, it's important to find a way to access it that works for you. No two people will do so in exactly the same way. And don't let anybody tell you that you need to spend hours, days, weeks, or even years searching. The trustworthy insight you receive in an instant is no less valuable than the ones you develop over a lifetime. When you use your gift of Trust, you can be sure that whatever you're sensing is the right thing for that moment.

When I talk about using my gift of Trust in my workshops, people often ask me, "How can you be sure it's the promptings of God you're sensing and not just something out of your own head?" And I answer honestly: I'm not sure. However, experience has taught me that Trust has three identifiable characteristics:

1. Whatever I am thinking, saying, or doing is not making me restless, nervous, or overly excited. If I find myself trying to force or convince another person of something, I'm usually cut off from Trust. Trust *always* comes from love, without conditions.

2. My thoughts, words, or actions flow. I am calm, astonishingly articulate, or things work out simply, easily, and quickly.

3. I have no regrets afterward. There is nothing I would think, say, or do differently.

Although I do meditate and/or pray daily, I often find myself in situations where I don't have time to do either, even though I sense I need my gift of Trust. So instead, one of the things I have found that works for me is to stop for an instant, ask myself, "What would love do now?" and pause for about another thirty seconds before proceeding. I don't always get clear "directions" on what to do, but because I have made a point of choosing a place of peace from which to enter the moment, I am usually more aware of how I can lovingly support or enhance my own or another's actions. I wish I could say that I do this all the time, but get real. In any given day, I may do this once or twice. At this point, I will almost always do so if things are getting stressful, because then I truly know that I have fallen out of touch with my gifts.

Here are the three steps I use:

1. Make a decision to use your gift of Trust.

2. Stop whatever it is you're doing.

3. Close your eyes, state your intention, and take one or more deep breaths to clear out some of the tension that is blocking the expression of your gift. Wait another fifteen to thirty seconds or so before proceeding.

The state-your-intention part is a little tricky at first, but you'll get the hang of it. (Note: See Chapter 11 for more about using your gift of Intention.) Start by simply telling yourself that you want to feel good. All day long, we're observing things that make us feel bad and invite us to try to change them. We want to save the world from violence, or end hunger, or house the homeless. On a smaller scale, we may want to cheer up a sick friend, find a way to pay our bills, or make love to our spouses. Usually we don't know exactly how to make that happen in our busy, overextended lives. So if you simply state "I want to feel good," trust eventually will give you that "Ah-ha!" moment that will deliver what you want. And in the meantime, you've taken a strong step to stem the flow of negativity in your life.

You can also state things like "I wish I could help/be of service" or "I'd love to feel better about how I handle money." Again, experiment. You'll soon discover which intentions feel right to you.

If you're not a close-your-eyes type of person, here are a few more one-minute relaxers you can try:

1. Open your favorite book at random. Read for one minute. See what message is there for you.

2. Eat a miniature dark chocolate candy bar very, very slowly. I am not kidding about this. Pure, dark chocolate (sorry, milk chocolate lovers) has copper in it, and research has now proven that a little bit of this every day actually improves the electrical connections in your heart. If your heart is sound, it makes sense to think that more oxygen is being delivered to your brain, and you'll think more clearly. Plus, the smooth sweetness is very soothing for a lot of people. Enjoy!

3. Sip a glass of water. Think of it as giving your insides a shower. Remember, sip; don't gulp. Put all your attention on the sipping as you're doing it, thus taking your mind off your worries and problems.

4. Stare. Find a window or an object, and stare at it. Again, this has the effect of taking your mind off what is bothering you and bringing you back to center, like putting blinders on a horse. I tell people to stare at their pinky nail, because it's readily available

and it's small. When they do, funny things start to happen. They not only lose their worries, but often they run right out and get a manicure afterward!

5. Doodle. Try it a little differently: Put the pen in your subdominant (weaker) hand. Let it roam all over the paper. Don't watch. See what you've got when the minute is up. Supposedly this is one way to access your subconscious.

6. Hum. Any song will do—stick with the first one that comes to mind. Humming, I have found, is very internal. It tickles your insides and puts a kind of Cheshire cat grin on your face, which again tends to cast off negativity and make you more receptive to the good within.

7. Hug. A one-minute hug is long, so make sure that whoever you're hugging is someone you already trust. With it comes a sense of safety and peace that stimulates the gift of Trust.

8. Laugh. Keep a repertoire of story-type jokes you can tell in a minute or less. If you need a resource, get a book or check the Internet. Again, you will be losing the negativity and "switching on" the love.

9. Listen to music. Preferably not heavy metal or anything sad. I keep a library of piano, flute, and other solos around and use those to reset my mood.

10. Walk. Walk around the office, the house, the block—wherever you can go in one minute. If you're truly trapped, stretch at your desk or in a chair or bed instead. Just by changing your position, you've altered the way things have been flowing. And when

you put your physical form in motion, no matter how limited, you're stirring up energy. Move slowly. Enjoy.

11. Smile. Did you know that if you smile fifteen times a day, you'll be 20 percent healthier than the rest of the American population? Sad, but true. Put a smile on your face for one full minute. Either you'll start to roar at the silliness of it, or everybody else will because you look a little nuts. But one thing you'll notice: when you smile, whoever sees it is bound to smile back. And when the minute is up, it's hard to *stop* smiling. Watch what good that does!

12. Smell something wonderful. Keep an orange or some fresh flowers on your desk, or go outside to the nearest bakery or pizza place. Today you can even buy tiny inhalers—I keep one in my desk drawer called "Joy," which contains the aromas of Bulgarian roses among other sweet scents. You could even spray some perfume or cologne on your wrists and breathe that in for a minute.

Another way to use your gift is to trust someone else. If a loved one makes a promise to you, believe him or her. If you lend out a piece of personal property, expect to get it back or to have something better enter your life at a later time if you don't. One important note, however: Use your gift this way only if it feels right to you. If you start feeling worried, nervous, or upset, try one of the other methods, or this one might backfire on you.

Remember—the gift of Trust is not a momentary thing. It's like receiving a plant. The more you tend to it, talk to it, expose it to daylight, and feed it, the better it will grow. Enjoy it not only for what it is now but for what it can and will be in the future.

CHAPTER NINE

. . . .

The Gift of Character

AS I SAID in the introduction, the most remarkable thing about my flood experience was how liberating it was in many ways. Overnight, I was freed from all of my roles and the expectations that went with them. Most of these expectations were not from other people but things I demanded of myself, beliefs, and actions I assumed would make me "good" at the roles I played.

For the first few days after we evacuated, I felt suspended in time and space. From this semidetached place, I wasn't living the life I'd known, but I could see it clearly, like mentally watching a rerun of myself in a sitcom. Some of it was funny, some sad, some just so-so. But imagining what I would have been doing, saying, or thinking if things were "normal" made me sure of just one thing: I had created all of it by how I defined myself.

I found myself wondering "Who is Robin now?" Thanks to the emergency conditions, I was eating things "Robin" would never normally eat (especially since it was Passover, when Jewish diets are extraordinarily restricted) and doing things "I" would never do, such as sleeping without an alarm clock or pressing a fresh shirt for myself every day. (Since I only had two with me, that was as much a matter of necessity as choice. Still, it was fun dragging out the ironing board every day, especially knowing that I could have just as easily gone around rumpled and disheveled and nobody would have cared.) I was breaking a lot of my own rules, not rebelliously but almost instinctually. Since there was nothing I was expected to do, I just did whatever felt right to me. And I liked the person who was emerging as a result.

TRY ON A NEW DEFINITION OF SELF

I decided to try on a new persona. I looked around to see how other people were defining or redefining themselves and experimented with what appealed to me. "Robin the Victim" didn't suit me at all, nor did "Robin the Survivor." Both seemed to come with this dark cloud hovering nearby, and instead of feeling ennobled, I felt depressed as I swapped stories of suffering with others.

Then I tried "Robin the Dorm Queen," which was actually kind of fun. We had the supreme good fortune of securing a furnished apartment for the six weeks of our evacuation, thanks to our close friends Hal and Kathy, who found a studio for themselves in the same building. I liked running down the hall in my bare feet to knock on their door. Neither of our apartments came with much in the way of accessories, such as dishes, pots, and pans. When my birthday came, Kathy made an incredible lasagna by cooking each ingredient one at a time in the same pot. Sally and her daughter drove down from their lake home, Steve and I brought our own plates and forks, and we all had a marvelous time.

But "Robin the Dorm Queen" wasn't a permanent role; I knew we'd have to go home sooner or later. So I tried "Relaxed Robin," the one who refused to get all worked up about anything. This was an interesting switch for someone who usually tried to control everything. Away went the anger, the raw fire that would demand that things be done a certain way by a certain time.

This one wasn't a bad choice, mostly because it fit the situation well. With close to 20,000 homes damaged in the two towns, local contractors were overwhelmed, if you could even find one. Start yelling or demanding, and they'd hang up the phone. And who could blame them? Still, I found myself amazed at my own comments, such as "I understand how hard things are for you right now. I know you'll get to it as soon as you can." Although I could see "the organizer" in me at work, I couldn't see any of the boss, the anguished director, or the race runner. What was interesting was that the less demanding I became, the quicker things tended to fall into place. Instead of everything being about "me" or "us," it was obvious that there was a much bigger picture to be considered here and that a nicer, more patient, more cooperative and appreciative Robin would be welcome.

But "Relaxed Robin" only went so far. My "to do" list was substantial, and I was spending long hours at my desk. So I added "Focused Robin," someone totally unlike the old me, the penultimate juggler who always had her mind on fifteen things at once. In this case, I kept my attention on whatever was the project of the moment, taking it as far as it could go for that day before moving on. Again, I liked the results, so I worked on developing that part of my character.

Finally I added in "Loving Robin." I have always been an affectionate person, so I wasn't looking for that. Rather, I tried to create—or, should I say, allow—more passion for what I was doing and the people for whom I was doing it. Although I wondered if this persona would conflict with "Relaxed Robin," I found that it didn't. If anything, it made me more sincere and secure, because I knew whom I truly valued and what I could do for myself and them.

This new Robin rarely felt tired. I was incredibly busy— much more so than before, in many ways. But instead of feeling worn out by all I had to do, every connection I made and complication I encountered energized me. I was doing things I had done before, such as fielding phone calls for our synagogue, calling my writing subjects for interviews, and making repair arrangements for our house. But I was doing them in a new way, and I knew that although we would go back, things would never be the same again. Not just the house or the neighborhood, but me. I liked this new, easier-going Robin a lot better than the old "Damn the torpedoes, and full steam ahead!" one, and I wanted to know more about her.

THE PERSON YOU ALWAYS WANTED TO KNOW

That's when I met the gift of Character. I say "met" rather than "discovered," because Character is not simply a matter of values, as most people believe. Instead, when you choose to use your gift of Character, it is like being introduced to someone you've always wanted to meet. You know who he or she is and what he or she does, but Character goes deeper than that. The gift of Character is not just what you believe is right or wrong but how the person who emerges thinks, feels, talks, and acts. Many people hold values that are never expressed; the gift of Character puts what you believe into action so that you and others can see that good is not just an idea, it's *real*.

One attribute of the gift of Character is consistency, because when you use this gift, what you think, say, do, believe, and value all harmonize perfectly. Use it, and you will "walk your talk," with the added depth of knowing that what you say will honestly and correctly express the best in you. With the gift of Character, you are not one thing to one person and another thing to someone else. You do not wear a smile simply to keep everyone happy, nor do you regale others

144 • ROBIN L. SILVERMAN

with your troubles to make them see or wallow in your miserable point of view. Who you are is also who you want to be.

The feeling of peace that you get with this gift is incredible. When you use it, you will soon learn the magic word "no." Most of us—particularly the women reading this—are afraid to say no to anyone. But when the "no" comes from your gift of Character, it does not offend or alienate anyone, because you are actually saying "yes" to something more important—the person you have always wanted to be. The gift of Character takes a lot of the resentment and frustration out of life, because if you honor the gift, you will rarely find yourself in a situation you dislike.

The gift of Character answers the question, "Who do I want to be now?" Children use it constantly, when they use their imaginations to pretend they are someone else. It works pretty much the same way for adults. If you don't like who you are or who you have become, the first step is to decide to change that. Then you ask Character's question. Like me, you can look around you and try on several different personas—or pieces of them—that appeal to you. You also can go at the gift negatively, saying "This is absolutely, positively *not* who I want to be." If you go at it that way, however, be sure to ask the alternate question, "Who *do* I want to be?"

Then give it a go. Shakespeare said, "All the world's a stage and all the people merely players." But life is not a show without a director. Although God is the executive producer, each one of us gets to be our own scriptwriter and director. In other words, when we use our gift of Character, we can clearly decide who we want to be. By thinking, talking, and acting as we believe that person would, we become them.

For example, once I decided not to be a restless, argumentative, controlling player, I was drawn toward becoming kinder, more focused, and more loving. I looked around me for examples of people who got what they wanted by the power of attraction, not force. I found myself intuitively evaluating my thoughts and actions by asking myself "Is this what a kind/focused/loving person would think in these circumstances? Is this what she would say or do?" When the answer was "No!" (as it often was, especially at the beginning), I asked, "Then what would she think/say/do instead of this?" The answer always came, and I altered my behavior. In time, as both my confidence and my peace of mind grew, I found myself attracting better work assignments, living with a happier, healthier family, and having the ability to move to a new home with a minimum of emotional trauma.

STOP STRUGGLING, START LIVING

Until I discovered the gift of Character, I often wondered why things didn't go the way I wanted them to. Like most people, I felt that struggle was a great way to develop character. What I didn't realize was that struggle only makes you weary, frustrated, and angry, which didn't appeal to me at all. Instead, I found that the clearer I became about who I wanted to be, the more energy I had for the efforts I was making. I was still working "hard," but now it was *for* what I knew instinctively was right, not *against* something I thought was wrong.

One of the best illustrations of this definition of Character was presented on a TV biography of the actor Cary Grant. He was born Archibald Leach to parents of low to modest means. But a severely limited, disciplined life didn't appeal to him, and he ran away with the circus when he was a teen. Although his father found him and reenrolled him in school, Archie left home again and came to the United States. Here he modeled himself after actors Douglas Fairbanks and Noel Coward, two of the most sophisticated men of his day. By imagining himself as a suave gentleman of sophistication, means, and grace, he eventually became one. However, he never lost the comic sense he had developed in the circus, and some of his most beloved motion pictures are the ones where he plays the dignified fool. But he often said in interviews that he chose his "character" by playing the "part" until his dream of who he could be eventually became real.

Pop singer Madonna did the same thing. She went to New York City almost broke at the start of her career. But as she stood at Times Square during those early days, she was certain that someday she would stand on that same corner waving to tens of thousands of cheering fans. Again, in a television biography, Madonna's friends were quoted as saying that from the start, she acted like the successful performing artist she eventually became. There was never a moment when she wasn't "playing the part," including something as simple as when a friend combed her hair for her. Madonna "made believe" she was having her hair readied by a professional hairdresser for an appearance onstage. And one of the reasons for her continuing success is her ability to "reinvent" herself over and over, forever capturing the imaginations and attention of her audiences.

REINVENTION IS NOT ALWAYS NECESSARY

While the gift of Character can be used to reinvent yourself throughout your life, it also can be used to stay true to who you know yourself to be already. In this case, you are not acting a part, and there's no need to wait to reveal to others who you truly are. People who use the gift this way usually are not even conscious of doing so. They think, talk, and act the way they do because it simply doesn't occur to them to behave any other way. Usually they are remarkably unself-conscious and gracious toward others because they are neither judging nor feeling as if they are being judged. They simply are who they are.

This is the goal of using the gift of Character—to become, well, *yourself,* without worries or regrets. Some people do it naturally, and others, as I suggested earlier, have to play with it a bit. Either way, you have a lifetime to get good at it. There are no two humans who are completely identical in soul, spirit, and purpose. Each of us has a reason to be here, if for nothing else than to keep things interesting for everyone else. Think of how dull life would be if we were nothing more than clones of one another. After a while, you'd get bored talking to you!

One of the things I noticed in my search is that those who use the gift naturally and without a lot of conscious thought tend to be over age forty. Some have said that it's because by the time you are forty you've already become everything you're ever going to be. I don't agree with that, because it's obvious that people do a lot of character experimentation in their twenties and thirties. If they haven't gotten too stubborn by the time they're in their forties and fifties, they have a pretty good idea of what roles and personality traits *don't* work for them physically, spiritually, or materially. That makes them ready to change. Midlife crisis, anyone? And, as I discovered from my own experience, sometimes a life circumstance forces you to change, regardless of your age.

I've also been told that the best time in our lives is after age seventy or before age ten, because those are the only years when we don't care what other people think about us. Using our gift of Character, we don't have to waste the years in between. We can become peaceful with who we are and reinvent ourselves if circumstances demand it. That's what Esther did.

ESTHER'S STORY

Esther is an eighty-six-year-young widow who lost a leg to vascular disease. In spite of a bad hip and a weak shoulder, two independent teams of orthopedists declared her an "excellent" candidate for a prosthesis. I went to see her to ask her why the doctors were so enthusiastic about her chances for success with an artificial leg, in spite of her physical limitations.

When I walked into her room at the nursing home, she wasn't there. However, a book on how to surf the Internet lay on her bed, which piqued my attention. Obviously, this was a woman who was interested in learning and trying new things. A short time later, she entered the room in a wheelchair. She was small and frail, looking not at all like someone who could manage an artificial leg.

"Mrs. Qualey," I asked respectfully, "why do the doctors all feel that you'll succeed with a prosthesis?"

"Well, dear," she said quietly but resolutely, "I'm pretty determined. When I want something, I usually get it."

She sat up straighter in her chair. "You see, eight years ago [when she was seventy-eight], I was making jelly for my children and grandchildren when I ran out of lids for the jelly jars. So I got in my car to drive to the store to get some more.

"When I came around this one corner, the door of the car fell open. I reached for it, of course, but then I fell out of the car!" She laughed. "So there I was, sitting on the pavement, rubbing my head, when all of a sudden, the car comes backward and rolls over my foot!" She laughed again. "Now I'm rubbing both my head and my foot, but I notice that the car is still rolling and going down the hill. Well, I couldn't let that happen, so I got up and ran to it as best I could. [At this point, I imagined her holding her head and dragging her damaged foot behind her, which was quite a mental picture.] And you know what? I caught up to it!

"Well, once I was back in the car," she said matter-of-factly, "I figured I might as well go down to the store, get the jelly jar lids, and finish the jelly. So that's what I did."

I was dumbstruck. "Mrs. Qualey!" I exclaimed. "What about your head and your foot?"

She chuckled. "Oh, yes. *That,*" she said, like it was some kind of petty annoyance. "Well, I went to the doctor the next day. And he patted me on the head and turned my foot around, and I was all fine again."

As I sat there in total shock, the story of writer Lillian Hellman flashed in my mind. She had the uncanny ability to remove herself mentally from the reality of a situation. As she lay dying, a nurse stopped her lover before he could enter the room. "I have to warn you, it's very bad," she said, going into lengthy detail about how Miss Hellman's heart, eyes, kidneys, and more were all failing. The lover nodded his understanding and then proceeded to her bed.

"How are you, Lillian?" he asked gently.

"Terrible," she replied. He waited to hear a long discourse about her pain and symptoms. But instead, she said, "I have the worst writer's block I've ever had!"

The end of Esther's story is that, unfortunately, the prosthesis was not a success. However, she was very peaceful about it: "I wouldn't have been happy with myself unless I tried." Instead, she became what one nursing home worker called "the Queen of the Walkers." No wheelchair-bound cripple, she got back up on her one good foot again and successfully navigates the halls to the beat of her own personal drum. Determination and a good sense of humor are part of her gift, and they've helped her weather the changes brought on by her medical condition.

The gift of Character shines through even the most seemingly ordinary moments. There are rare people who use their favorite character traits so consistently that they are totally unaware they are doing so. Their inner light shines through without effort or filtration. I discovered this when I met Roland.

ROLAND'S STORY

"Come to graduation with me. It will be fun," said my friend Toby, the wife of Ken Baker, then the president of the University of North Dakota. "There's a luncheon beforehand, with some great surprises. You'll love it."

So I polished up my pumps, put on my best suit, and went. Toby was right; the luncheon was something special. With less than fifty people, it was relatively intimate, considering the celebrity nature of two of the guests. The first was Roland Flint, poet laureate of the state of Maryland since 1995. A professor of writing and literature at Georgetown University, Flint had come back to Grand Forks to receive an honorary degree from UND, his alma mater. The second was author Garrison Keillor, one of Flint's best friends, who "came along for the ride."

After the last dessert plate was removed, President Baker stood up and invited Flint to share a poem with the group. Flint is a solid block of a man, a quiet but firm presence who calls his poems "user friendly." Now he stood in the center of an attentive room. The guests put down their coffee cups and turned to face him, and as silence reigned, he began to speak.

It is hot today, dry enough for cutting grain,

And I'm drifting back to North Dakota
Where butterflies are all gone brown with wheat
*   dust.*

And where some boy,
Red-faced, sweating, chafed,
Too young to be dying this way,
Steers a laborious, self-propelled combine
Dreaming of cities, and blizzards—
And airplanes.

With the white silk scarf of his sleeves
He shines and shines his goggles,
He checks his meters, checks his flaps,
Screams contact at his dreamless father.
He pulls back the stick,
Engines roaring.
And hurtles into the sun.

© Roland Flint. Used with permission.

When he finished, no one breathed. He had captured not only the harvest experience but the dreams of a young boy. And, for that matter, the hearts of everyone listening. The sound of applause woke up all of us. As he returned to his seat, one person stood to honor him, then another, and another, until the entire room was on its feet, celebrating the man who had stirred our souls.

As he passed by my seat, the only word that came to mind was "Wow!" Suddenly I wanted to be a middle-age man who knew how to chisel words of coal into diamonds. I wanted my work to be published in the *Atlantic Monthly*. I wanted to be known as someone who took a discipline that confounded most people and made it accessible. I stood there clapping for as long as I could without embarrassment.

When it came time to leave, Flint and Keillor stationed themselves at opposite sides of the door. I wasn't sure what to say to Keillor, although I admired his work and the joy it brought others. But I knew what I wanted to say to Flint. I went to his side of the door and extended my hand.

"Thank you," I said, not knowing a better way to express not only my appreciation for his reading but my awe. "That was the most beautiful description of the harvest I've ever heard."

I expected him to say "Thank you" and look past me to whoever was either next in line or more important. But he didn't. Instead, he wrapped his two warm, stocky hands around my cool, skinny one and looked me in the eye.

"Tell me your name," he said.

The question was so unexpected that I almost forgot the answer. "Uh, it's Robin."

"Well, Robin," he said, "why are you here today? Are you receiving an honorary degree, too?"

"Not exactly," I said, trying to think of a clever way to say that it was an honor to escort Toby to the graduation ceremony.

He didn't skip a beat. "Are you faculty?"

I finally found my breath, and my smile. Although I had done some occasional lecturing for the university, I knew that was not why I had been invited. "No—I'm actually just here with a friend."

He smiled, too. "Well, I want you to know that your compliment means a great deal to me. Thank you for coming over to tell me."

I think I nodded, then moved on to give someone else a chance to talk to this extraordinary man. Besides the obvious skill he had at his craft, his gift of Character was flawless. I later talked to the organizer of the event, who laughed when she heard my story. "Oh, he's like that with everybody," she said. "He makes you feel like you're the only person in the world when you talk to him."

I thought of all the times I had scoffed when someone tried to give me a compliment or never learned the name of a stranger who gave a bit of kindness to me. And it made me realize that each of us is more than what we do or how we define ourselves; we are the love that placed us here in the first place. I later learned that Flint described poetry as "a quick way to the sources of the spirit," and it was obvious from his demeanor both in the spotlight and out that he was coming from that sure, tender place that most of us long for but never reach. He knew, surely and absolutely, who he was and wanted to be with others. To me, his unassuming, welcoming character was a gift.

The last story I'd like to share about the gift of Character is one I heard told by motivational speaker Kyle Rote, Jr. Rote was describing a friend of his, a man who desperately wanted to be a professional baseball player but lost both legs in the Vietnam war. When this brave man woke up in the hospital, he was glad to be alive, but sad that his potential career as a baseball player was over. Still, he found himself instinctively offering a prayer. "Well, God, what are you going to do with a legless baseball player?"

The next thing that happened was that a nurse came in and handed him some light weights. "You're going to need these," she said, "to build your upper body strength."

Like a professional sports figure, he worked out daily. Eventually he graduated from hand weights to barbells, and in time he became a weight-lifting champion in his weight class. Ironically, jealous competitors took the title from him, insisting he was not wearing one of the pieces of regulation gear at the time of his win: shoes.

Although he "lost" that inning, he went on to win the "game" by learning to walk on his arms. He'd put blocks under his hands, steel his muscles, and swing his torso to move forward. At first, he couldn't finish a single track-length. But soon he was cruising long distances.

Finally he decided he would "walk" all the way from California to the Vietnam Veterans Memorial in Washington, D.C. It took him three years, but he did it.

The legless baseball player scored the winning run in the World Series of life.

PEACE PROGRESS STEP 9

. . . .

Haul Out the Mental Trash

If you are already using your gift of Character in a way that feels peaceful to you, skip this section. If, however, life has handed you a circumstance where you'd like to reinvent yourself (or possibly stay true to yourself in spite of what life has handed you), read on.

Because of the preponderance of negativity in our thinking, it's much easier to determine what we *don't* like, either about ourselves or others. So get out a piece of paper, and write at the top: "What I absolutely, positively *do not* want to be!"

Then start writing, keeping your list in a single column down the left-hand side of the page. Think about all the things you've seen others do that really annoy or upset you. Put down what you are sure does not work for people, what seems to trip them up or keep them from getting what they say they say they want. Here is what your list might look like:

What I absolutely, positively do *not* want to be:
Angry
Judgmental
Stubborn
Arrogant
Flighty
Jealous

Fearful
Gossipy
Passive
Hostile

Keep going until you feel you have exhausted all you want to express. You may cringe a bit to realize that this is likely all you have been noticing about yourself or others up to this point. But relax; that's about to change.

Now, across the page from your first list, make a second one: "What I absolutely, positively *do* want to be." Then write words that are the exact opposite of the first ones you wrote. So your paper might look like this:

What I absolutely, positively do *not* want:	What I absolutely, positively *do* want:
Angry	Peaceful/content
Judgmental	Accepting
Stubborn	Flexible
Arrogant	Humble
Flighty	Grounded
Jealous	Loving
Fearful	Fearless
Gossipy	Self-aware
Passive	Active
Hostile	Supportive

Now take your second list and rewrite it on a clean sheet of paper. Destroy the first one. At the top of the new page, write the question: "Who do I know or admire who has some of these traits?"

Think for a minute. Start with your immediate circle of family, friends, and neighbors. Then spread out to people you know at work, not only at your present job but any you may have had in the past. Think about teachers you had in school, and see if any of them made a positive impression on you in any of the categories you listed. Then add in people you may encounter in daily life: shopkeepers and clerks, servers in restaurants, the bagger at the grocery store. Everyone is good at heart; some simply demonstrate it more than others.

From there, go to celebrities and political figures you admire, including those from the past who may be dead and gone. Fictional characters might work for you, too, either from books or the movies. You're also welcome to put religious figures on your list, such as Christ, Mary, Moses, Mohammed, Buddha, or any of the prophets or psalmists. Make your list as long and comprehensive or as short and simple as you like. It's good to place at least one name by each character trait so that you know you have them all covered. (You also can describe total strangers, many of whom were my best teachers during our evacuation.)

Next, close your eyes and ask your soul, "Which of these traits would serve me best right now?" When you open your eyes, one will almost surely pop out at you, along with the corresponding name. Let's say you pick "Supportive," and alongside it are "Mom and Dad." Go back in your memory and think of one or more instances that made you come to that conclusion. Replay the moment in your mind until you can clearly see what they say and how they act. In your way of thinking, how do supportive people behave?

When you know, you are ready to use your gift to create a "character" who is supportive of others. Prepare by mentally practicing what you will think, say, and do the next time you encounter someone who could use your support. You can even practice in front of a mirror if you like, or test your theory by talking it through with a friend. As you're doing so, ask yourself: "Is this what a supportive person would think? Is this what a supportive person would say? Is that what a supportive person would do?" Your gift of Trust will kick in, and you'll know by how you feel whether you're on the right track.

When you feel somewhat confident (don't worry; the more you use your gift, the quicker and easier this gets), affirm, "I am a supportive person." Tell yourself that many times every day, and act the part whenever you get the chance, which is likely to be more often than you think. Once you've chosen to use your gifts, you will begin attracting circumstances that will allow you to do so. Take advantage of as many of these opportunities as you can.

Eventually, the wonderful, happy, contented, lively characters you "portray" won't feel like fiction to you. You will be so practiced in the character traits you want that they will become natural. You will have manifested a "new you," although really it was simply someone who was deep inside you all along. And when you start living that truth, that you are, indeed, better than you thought, you will be well on your way to a more peaceful life.

P.S. If you create a character you do not like or that doesn't work as well as you thought, try again. You might want to use your gift of Love, to be sure you're noticing the *best* in others. Make sure your choices are what make you feel good, not guilty, as in "a good/successful/happy person *ought* to have this trait." Forget what you may have learned in the past, and work from how you feel right now, in the present. You can't get it wrong; some character traits will simply work better for you than others will. Remember that no matter where you are, you can use "I know what I absolutely, positively do *not* want to be" at any time to help you script a new direction for yourself.

. . . .

CHAPTER TEN

The Gift of Thanks

THERE IS NOT one among us who did not learn the response of "thank you" as a child. In fact, usually it's one of the first things we are taught. "Say 'thank you,' " our parents insist as they are handing us the cookie or blanket we are demanding. "Kay-koo" is one of our earliest phrases, and we are expected to use it and praised heartily for doing so.

But there is a problem. Just as quickly as we learn to say "thank you," we also learn that it always seems to come with a catch. We don't say it *until* we have been given something. It's always used in some sort of exchange. You give/I get/I say "Thank you"/you say "You're welcome." We all know the drill, which feels desperately incomplete if even one piece of it is missing. We wait to offer our thanks, selfishly hoarding these precious words until we have proof that another person has deemed us worthy of what we want.

Thus, "thank you" becomes more of an obligation than a spontaneous eruption of joy. Although whatever we have been given probably was meant to help us feel good, we're supposed to say "thank you," whether we liked what we were given or not. If we don't, we are considered unmannerly, ungrateful, rude, or depressed.

The more we use "thank you" this way, the more it loses its original intent, which is to make some generous soul feel good. After a while, we never know if the person saying it truly means it or not. And it's a double-edged sword: If a person doesn't say or express thanks at all, we're annoyed. Worse, we've learned to use "thank you" sarcastically, as in "Thanks for nothing!" Or "Thanks a ton for dumping all that work on me." "Thank you" has become something of a burden in modern society and could really use replacement.

That's why I was delighted when I discovered the gift of Thanks. After the flood, there were literally tens of thousands of reasons for all of us to be thankful. First and most important, because not one single person died in the flood. Second, because as we returned to our damaged homes, businesses, schools, houses of worship, and community, people from all over the country rushed in to help us recover. Because virtually every home in our two cities was damaged, there was no way we could help one another. Without the kindness of strangers, many, many people would never have been able to go back home, or to school, work, or worship.

People from every state sent money in every conceivable form—some anonymously, as in our "angel" (later discovered to be McDonald's heiress Joan Kroc), who gave millions to help individual families recover, some taping allowance quarters to sheets of lined paper or putting a sticky note that said "Hang in there!" on a $50 check. The money came to the mayors of the two towns, Pat Owens and Lynn Stauss, to our houses of worship, to our educational foundation, and more. It came through the Red Cross and the United Way. For months and months, it kept coming and coming.

And that wasn't all. The people came, too. I will never forget the first day we came home to start pumping out our basement. The city still had no power, lights, or water, and we were hungry after hours at work. We knew nothing was open, but we drove around anyway, hoping to spot the Red Cross truck. Instead, on this gray, thirty-eight-degree day, we smelled something barbecuing. "How clever!" I said to Steve. Our own grill had floated away during the flood; I wondered if whoever was cooking would be willing to share some of their bounty, since there was barely anyone around.

We followed the smell, which led us into the parking lot of the senior citizen's center. The center was closed, of course, but there in the parking lot were two camping trailers, about a half-dozen barbecue grills, and a handful of people holding burgers and brats in their mittened hands. We walked over, and a pink-cheeked, middle-age man waved us closer.

"Hungry?" he asked. "We've got plenty!"

"Where did you come from?" I asked, noticing what looked like a pretty professional setup.

"We're a Lion's Club from Wisconsin," he answered. "We thought you all might enjoy this."

We did. To this day, I can still taste that burger.

There were too many other generous gestures to recount them all here, starting with the rock band and clothing designer who helped create a prom for our kids to the almost 20,000 volunteers who came from all over the country to help us clean up and repair our buildings. As I write this, more than two years after the disaster, many, many people are still giving their time and money to help Greater Grand Forks recover.

A NEW DEFINITION OF THANKS

There have been countless "thank yous," of course, most of which have been totally sincere. Using the old definition, we received abundantly, and we were all abundantly grateful for it. But the gift of Thanks began to appear when I heard people say "This was an answer to my prayer." For the first time, I realized that many people had been saying "Thank you, God, for providing for me" long before there was any evidence of that being true. It never occurs to us to say thanks in *anticipation* of something good, to acknowledge the desires of our own hearts with the gratitude we reserve for after we receive the attentions of others. This is thanks not as obligation or exchange but thanks as creation—or rather, cocreation. With this gift, "Thanks" is a way of saying "This would be good," and we feel the truth of that. And when what we are thankful for does indeed appear, the spontaneous, joyous response is "What a blessing!"

When God created the world, at the end of each day, He looked at what He'd created and said, "It is good." He didn't say, "It is bad, and I think I'll do it over." Instead, He created man and woman to enjoy it. And when the world was complete, God created the Sabbath day. Jewish people think of Shabbat as a bride, something incredibly beautiful that ushers in a day of joy. The Sabbath has become a day when we pause to appreciate where we have been in the past week and gain perspective on what we may give and receive in the week ahead. It's no wonder that God didn't just say the Sabbath was good; God blessed it. And by doing so, God made it holy, something akin to spiritual perfection. As a result, there are few among us who don't think of the Sabbath as a day of peace. Blessing your own creations feels just as good.

When you bless your heart's desire, you go beyond saying "This is good," to proclaiming "This is perfect!" It's another way of saying "Just what I always wanted!" Blessings are dreams come true, love made real, joy incarnate. Blessing is how you demonstrate joy. Receiving one or being told you are one to someone else feels wonderful. And once you do, it's practically impossible not to want to be one or give one to someone else.

This is the gift of Thanks. It goes beyond acknowledgment, gratitude, and obligation to awareness, delight, and contentment. It comes with a feeling of pure happiness that is temporary but memorable. The gift of Thanks is what you give, not what you get. It makes us feel very, very peaceful, even if just for a short while. But that's enough to make us want to use it again and again and again.

WHOM OR WHAT CAN YOU BLESS?

The gift of Thanks answers the question "Whom or what can I bless?" And what's interesting about this question is that we will have no idea of the answer until it is presented to us. The gift of Thanks keeps us in constant service to God by delivering us to one another. There is wonder in it, as we never know how our blessings will show up or where we are to distribute them once they do. By using this gift, we trust that we will simply be in the right place at the right time to receive what we—or someone else—needs. You will never fear lack again, nor will you doubt your worth or purpose here on Earth.

I have found several ways to bring this gift into use. The first and best way is to make a wish in the form of a prayer: "Thank you, God, for providing me with what I need right now." Remain still for a few moments after you have expressed your prayer, to offer your peacefulness "in exchange" for what you are about to be given. I've always felt that our misery does not serve God; it just gives Him more to do. Instead, it is our joy that brings God glory and makes the most of our limited number of days here on Earth. Even our ancient ancestors seemed to know this. Thousands of years ago, they did not bring their poor offerings to the temple; they brought only their best. Regardless of what might be happening in your life at the moment, bring your best to the moment of thanks.

You'll note that the prayer I suggest at the end of the chapter is open-ended. It does not ask for a specific thing to be delivered in a specific time or in a specific way. Instead, it focuses on the delivery of "what I need right now," which will likely take a form that will surprise you. You may or may not like it at first, thinking "This isn't what I prayed for!" But if step back and think about it, likely you will find that whatever you have received is absolutely perfect for you.

If you're the kind of person who likes more control, you might want to try a more childlike variation of praying with thanks: Make a wish. But this method comes with a warning: Be careful what you wish for. I once worked with a woman who wailed, "I wish I had a car that didn't have 180,000 miles on it!" When that one broke down, the next one she was offered had over 200,000 miles on it. (Later I jokingly suggested that she should have wished for a brand-new Jaguar.)

Most of us learned to keep our wishes to ourselves, being warned that they wouldn't come true if we shared them with others. But when it comes to using the gift of Thanks, I have found the opposite to be true. You simply make your wish out loud, thereby releasing a desire of your heart. (Do it when you're alone if you're self-conscious around others.) When it comes to wishes, the more specific, the better, but there's a caveat. If you make a wish, be careful not to counteract it immediately by thinking or saying "Wishes never come true." If you believe that, then this is not the way to use your gift. The speed with which your gift shows up depends on how clear you are about it. So if you are very, very clear about what you want and can truly say that receiving it feels good and right to you (imagine that you already have, and notice your emotions), then go for it.

The third and possibly best way to use the gift of Thanks is not to direct it consciously at all. In other words, ask for nothing and wish for nothing. Instead, using your gift of Trust, know that your "radio transmitter" to God is always switched "on" and that God's universe can hear you loud and clear without your having to say or do anything. To use your gift of Thanks this way, turn your focus outward and start paying attention to what's happening to you in your life. Likely you will see that reassurance is being given, doors are opening, and help is arriving without your specific request. You are being blessed, and the experience will feel holy to you, although possibly only in retrospect. This is what happened to Ellen.

ELLEN'S STORY

Ellen had been in the hospital for weeks, and there was no end in sight. She was grateful to be alive; she had narrowly escaped death from bacteria that swept through her flu-weakened body with a ferocity that forced a team of surgeons to remove most of the skin and tissue from one of her legs. Now she was faced with repeated skin-grafting surgery and months of rehabilitation. At age thirty-three all she wanted to do was go home to her husband and two young sons, ages one and four. But there was no chance of that at the moment.

Although Ellen used both prayer and visualization to aid her recovery, the days and nights dragged on wearily for her. She was beginning to feel frustrated that her life would never be the same again. Her doctors and nurses tried to reassure her that, in time, she would be able to live normally, but their words seemed hollow.

One day, as she lay in her hospital bed, a housekeeper entered her room. Ellen had seen her before but didn't know her name. They began to chat. The woman asked Ellen what church she attended, and they soon discovered that both were Catholic.

"I have some waters from Fatima," the woman said a little shyly. "My uncle gave them to me. I'd been saving them, but something told me you needed them. I'd like to give them to you . . . if you want them."

THE TEN GIFTS • 165

At first, Ellen didn't know what to think of the woman's offer. "But then it hit me," she said later. "Fatima—major miracles!" So she told the woman yes, she would very much like to receive her present.

The woman smiled nervously but happily. "I wanted to bring them with me, but I'm not a priest," she said, which made Ellen think. What would she do with the waters? Drink them? Ask her priest to anoint her? Pour them on her wounded leg?

"I don't work tomorrow," the woman said gently. "But I'll bring them by. See you then."

The next day the woman returned. She handed Ellen a book, *One Hundred Portraits of Christ.* There was a page folded down, but Ellen didn't open the book right away. (Later Ellen discovered that the chapter the woman had marked was on having the faith to heal yourself.) The woman had her hand wrapped tightly around something else. When she peeled back her fingers, there was a small clear vial with a white lid that looked something like an empty pill container. It had a piece of masking tape wrapped around it, upon which was typed "Fatima Water." The woman handed the tiny jar to Ellen.

Ellen looked at it with wonder. The water inside didn't even look particularly pure or clear. It was almost as if someone had run down to a stream and captured some of the flow as a keepsake of a happy day, or something like that.

Although the water seemed quite ordinary, Ellen knew that the woman's gesture was not. "I felt overwhelmed at the power of love and kindness from a stranger," she said. She looked at the woman gratefully. "I don't know what to say. Are you sure you want to give this up?"

The woman nodded. "It's for you." She paused, carefully considering what she would say next. "I've watched you deal with a lot of very difficult things, and it makes me want to handle my own life differently."

Ellen had never considered that her experience would

inspire others. "If you should ever need me, I'll be here for you," she said gently.

The woman smiled and then continued. "I don't want to offend you in any way," she said somewhat tentatively. "But did you know that wherever the heart of Mary and Jesus are, there is healing?" And with that, she walked over to the window. Lying on the sill was a red glass heart that a friend of Ellen's had given her. The woman took a greeting card she had brought and placed it behind the heart, blocking the sun. Suddenly Ellen saw light radiate from the heart. "It was the one and only time it happened," she admitted, marveling at what appeared to be a miracle of reassurance.

The woman drew nearer to Ellen's bed. "I also have something else for you, if you want to accept it," she said. Ellen nodded, and the woman handed her a pin adorned with the image of Raphael, the angel of healing. Ellen was astounded. "It was another confirmation," she said. "Nobody knew I had been praying to Raphael."

Ellen attached the pin to her hospital gown, and the woman left. After she had gone, Ellen turned the vial over and over in her hand. Was this water really from Fatima? And if it was, what was she supposed to do with it?

As she lay wondering, a familiar technician came in the room. "Do you know the name of the woman who was just in here?"

The technician shrugged. "When I looked in earlier, I was under the impression that she was one of your dearest friends."

She told the story again and again to every staff person who came in her room, but no one seemed to know the name of the mysterious woman. Ellen began to wonder if she had been visited by an angel, but the woman seemed too tentative for that. She put the vial on her bed tray and kept it there for days. Why had she received this now?

"Why me, God?" she asked one night, and the answer came in something of an epiphany. Ellen had been wondering if she would ever get well. Her despair was so deep that she knew that only God could understand her feelings about all she had been through. The mystery woman brought Ellen hope and the implied promise that she would recover, presented in a form that Ellen would accept and understand.

Ellen knew she had been blessed. And suddenly she knew exactly what to do with the precious vial: absolutely nothing. Regardless of the origin of the vial and its waters, their power lay not in the biology of the contents but in her belief and faith that healing was, indeed, not only possible but desirable. The gift was brought to remind her of that at exactly the moment she needed most. There was nothing she needed to "do" with the water except be with it and feel its legend and love flowing through her.

Ellen got out of the hospital and rehab several months later, and returned home to her family. She had a third child the following year, whom she calls her "miracle baby." Although her life is not exactly as it was before, it is good, and she is grateful to have her own leg rather than a prosthesis.

And the vial? It's tucked away in a special drawer where Ellen keeps her treasures. "I know exactly what it's for," she says confidently. "It was given to me so I could give it to someone else who needs its hope. And I will . . . when the moment is right."

Even though Ellen didn't "do" anything to activate her gift, it automatically delivered what she needed most. However, as she states, she will "pass on" the gift when the appropriate situation presents itself to her in her lifetime. This is an important component of the gift of Thanks. After you have received what you need—even if you didn't know you needed it or it came to you in a form you weren't expecting—you are meant to pass it on. Life isn't meant to be something that is hoarded, and there is no end to the bounty of God's grace and His universe. Not only are we gifted from within; we are continually being gifted from without. When we have more than we need, it is time to share so the blessing can be passed on . . . and on . . . and on . . . and on. . . .

Using the gift of Thanks usually involves taking action of some sort. Although Ellen will have to wait to give the vial away, she lives her gift every day by enjoying her time with her family to the fullest. She no longer takes any "normal" aspect of her life for granted, she says, and delights in what she is able to do in spite of her injured leg.

For other people, thanks is something you do for someone else that would be a blessing to him or her. That's how Debbie used her gift.

DEBBIE'S STORY

"I'm a cantorial soloist," Debbie said when she called. "Would you like me to chant at High Holy Day services?"

After the flood, I wasn't sure our synagogue building was even standing. And if it was, would we be able to have services in there by fall? I was a hundred miles away; how could I even answer the question?

"We're a tiny congregation," I said. "And after this, I don't know if we'll even have a building. It may not be worth your while to come up here."

"No, no—I'd love to come," she said emphatically. "There would be no charge."

No charge? This was hard to imagine. Our congregation had paid dearly over the years for a trained leader to take us through the numerous services of Rosh Hashanah, the Jewish new year, and Yom Kippur, the day of atonement. We put out the money because none of us could sing the complicated Hebrew prayers that characterize the holidays. Having a stunning voice chanting the traditional prayers was spiritually uplifting at a time when we felt we were making a fresh start on a new year and with God.

"Are you sure?" I asked, testing the waters again. "You want to come to Grand Forks for nothing?"

"Yes, I do," Debbie answered confidently. "You see, my family and I narrowly escaped a natural disaster last year, and I want to express my thanks by doing this."

"What happened?" I asked.

"Well, it was late—the middle of the night. My six-year-old son was in bed, and so were my husband and I. There had been storms in the area, but we didn't hear any sirens or warnings. Then, all of a sudden, we were awakened by this tremendous noise. It was roaring right by the bay window in our bedroom, and it was so loud that even though I was screaming, no one could hear my voice at all.

"I jumped out of bed and started running toward the door, and yelled for my husband to do the same. He couldn't hear me, but fortunately, he got out of bed. A few seconds later, a tornado ripped into the house, shattering the glass and spraying it right where we had been sleeping."

As I was exclaiming my horror, she continued. "We ran down the hall and got our son, and headed for the stairs. But it was like 'Where do I go? What do I do?' The tornado was literally chasing us through the house! Wherever we went, it went. We instinctively ran down the stairs, toward the front door. At that point, I figured we were dead. We were surrounded by glass, and there was nowhere else for us to go. We made it to the basement somehow and crouched in a closet, listening to windows exploding and draperies flapping in the wind. When it was over, we emerged from our hiding place to find the front of the house severely damaged, with rain and wind blowing through all the holes that had once been windows. But we were alive and unhurt."

Suddenly, our escape to Fargo didn't seem very dramatic

and our situation seemed far less perilous. "Was anybody in your neighborhood hurt?" I asked.

"Fortunately, no," she said. "The tornado took out our house and one other. It didn't hit the rest. But the problem was that our town had no sirens or warning system. One or two more seconds, and we would have been dead. So we lobbied, and now there's a system in place. Hopefully, no other family will ever be in as much jeopardy as we were."

"Wow! That's some story!" I exclaimed. "But you've already done the right thing by working to get the warning system in place. Why would you want to give away your services?"

"It's my way of saying thanks," she answered. "I'm grateful to be alive, and I'm happy to share my gift."

We made the necessary arrangements, and Debbie, her husband, and son all came to Grand Forks for Rosh Hashanah four months later. As it turned out, our synagogue building was heavily damaged but salvageable. Our kitchen, social hall, library, and utilities on the lower level had been destroyed, but we were able to get the building mucked out and electricity restored by the High Holy Days. We were happy—no, thrilled and relieved—to be together again, which would have been reason enough to be thankful.

Debbie's chantings were radiant, beautiful. They soared into the rafters and danced in our hearts. Her singing raised us up at a time when circumstances had brought us low. Her presence and her extraordinary voice made us feel that we had been blessed by God, not cursed by nature.

In each of these stories, the women felt as if they received a blessing, and each either intends to or already has passed it on to others. But there is one final way to use your gift of Thanks, and that is to give a blessing or be a blessing to someone else without necessarily having "received" one. I use "received" in quotes because life itself is the greatest blessing, so if you're reading this, you know you already have it.

PRAISE THE GOOD

The way to praise the good is to look at something you have created—from a child or a garden to a job well done at work—and praise it. God's way works for me, and I often find myself saying "This is good." Most of us destroy our own creations by declaring them puny, wrong, or not good enough, but there's no life in that. Instead, try admiring the people, things, and experiences you have gathered to you thus far. Bless them with your happiness at their presence in your life. For a few moments each day, be content with what you have. This does not mean that you can't or shouldn't want more out of life; that's what the gifts are for. But rather than waiting to be blessed when you arrive at the Pearly Gates, you can bring a little bit of heaven to Earth every day by blessing what is already yours.

If you've ever been confirmed, baptized, become a Bar or Bat Mitzvah, or been married in a Jewish or Christian religious ceremony, then you know the peace you feel at receiving the priestly blessing from the book of Numbers: "May the Lord bless you and keep you. May the Lord let His light shine upon you and be gracious unto you. May the Lord bestow His favor upon you, and grant you peace." Although most of us would feel awkward saying those exact words to another person, we can bless our families and friends and their efforts by offering our full, loving attention and wishing them well.

BE A BLESSING TO SOMEONE ELSE

Finally, you can be a blessing to someone who needs it. To do this, you'll need to use your gift of Trust, listening to your inner voice to know what's the best thing for you to do. Tune in, and then ask yourself the Gift of Thanks' question: "Whom or what can I bless?" As soon as you offer your service, God will show you who would most benefit from your help. Tread lovingly.

PEACE PROGRESS STEP 10

. . . .

Bless You!

Although there are several ways to access your gift of Thanks, there are really just two good ways to use it: to be a blessing either to yourself or to someone else. The first is actually the more important of the two, because if you feel shortchanged by life, what you offer to someone else will either be less than what you or the person wants, or possibly even harmful to the person and/or you. Conversely, if you feel abundantly blessed, you will likely feel peaceful in sharing or giving your blessings to someone else.

As stated earlier, one way to be a blessing to yourself is to bless or praise that which you have already gathered or created in your life. Unfortunately, most of us discount what we have by being dissatisfied with it. Our tendency is to notice what *isn't* right about our relationships, our homes, and our jobs—what in our estimation needs fixing or correcting. In my workshops, I do a simple exercise where I ask people if they've ever gone to the grocery store. After everyone in the room says yes, I ask them what they did there. Most of them say that they pick out foods that they want to eat and bring them home. At that point, I'll usually say "That's right! You never see anyone putting things in their cart and saying 'Oooo—I don't want to eat this and I hate the taste of that!' " So why is it, most of the time when we look in our bulging cupboards, we say "There's nothing to eat in this house"?

The tendency to overlook what is ours comes from our need to create. If everything were right, what would be left for us to do? How would we ever know how good we can be if nothing ever went wrong? On the other hand, how will we ever know peace unless we are willing and able to see— just for a moment—that something may be going very, very right for us?

So here are three prayers to help you use your gift of Thanks to bless your own life as it is and as it could be. Feel free to personalize them in your own religious tradition or in whatever spiritual way you are moved to do so.

This first prayer is for this moment. It will help connect you to whatever or whomever is with you now.

> *Source of Life,*
> *I come to this moment wide-eyed and ready.*
> *Show me the beauty I have brought into my life.*
> *Help me to appreciate the best of what is right here,*
>   *right now.*
> *Lift up my heart, so I may delight in this creation*
> *And bless it by saying with You,*
> *"This is good."*
> *Thank You, thank You for this rich reward,*
> *And for the peace of satisfaction.*
> *Amen.*

Note: *To bless a relationship or another person, substitute* "him" *or* "her" *for* "it," *and* "he" *or* "she" *for* "this."

The second prayer is useful if you want to bless a memory, something you have created in the past. It's a great tool to balance those moments when your life seems to be falling apart, because it reminds you that it wasn't always so. It's a helpful reminder of your roots when you are launching into something new and unknown, and can help you feel safe. Or you can use it strictly for pleasure's sake, to delight in your own sweet past.

Creator,
Be my guide as I travel back in time
To a moment I cherished.
Make it come alive again in my mind and my heart
So I may feel now as I felt then:
Happy, safe, and free.
Thank you for being present with me now and
before,
And for Your love, which is in every good moment.
May this memory be a blessing to me, and to You.
Amen.

Finally, if your dissatisfaction with the present and the past cannot be ignored, try this prayer. Conversely, it is also useful for when you are fully satisfied with both your past and present and are ready for something new and wonderful to enter your life. It does not specify what the "something wonderful" is. That's exactly the point. If you are deeply dissatisfied, you are more likely to know only what will make you less unhappy, not what will raise you up and make you feel truly peaceful. And if you already feel that you are abundantly blessed, it can be hard to imagine what would be more wonderful than what you already have. This prayer helps you "Let go and let God," as the saying goes. As you can see, it is worded as if the delight has already occurred, for indeed, in God's realm, it already has. Although it feels as if you are saying thanks "in advance," actually you are doing so in anticipation. Expect the best—it's on its way!

Sovereign of the universe,
I come to You now with a peaceful mind and a
thankful heart.
For You have delivered me to something more
wonderful than I could have ever imagined.
I am overwhelmed with excitement,
Overflowing with joy,
And passionate with delight.
My soul exalts in this new creation,
And every fiber of my being gives You thanks.
May this good be a blessing to me and all those
whose lives touch mine.
And may all praise go to You.
Amen.

If you'd rather live your prayers than say some, here are two dozen fun, easy ways for you to be a blessing to someone else. If you decide to do something from this list, do so without expecting a show of gratitude from the person for whom you are doing it. The thanks comes from within, acknowledging that you feel good because you did what you could.

1. Fill a basket with nonperishable food and place it anonymously on the doorstep of a needy family. (Ask around to see who needs help.)

2. Let a friend cry on your shoulder. Refrain from giving advice or saying "I told you so."

3. Encourage a child or, better yet, offer to mentor one.

4. Deliver a hot meal to a family who has a loved one who is sick at home or in the hospital.

5. Do the laundry of an elderly person or an invalid—including the ironing.

6. Shovel your neighbors' sidewalk and driveway, or mow their lawn while they are out of town.

7. Send money to someone you read about in the local paper who needs help. Do it anonymously.

8. Introduce two people you know would like each other (not necessarily for romantic reasons)

9. Refuse to believe the worst about someone.

10. Show up and offer a helping hand—especially if you are unexpected.

11. If someone you admire is going through a hard time, send a note of praise, illuminating his or her good qualities. Be specific about the traits you know the person has that will get him or her past the trouble with flying colors.

12. Offer to baby-sit on New Year's Eve or any other hard-to-find-a-sitter time. Or offer to do it anytime for any overworked and overwhelmed parents you know. Do it for free.

13. Visit someone who's sick or in the hospital more often than the person thought you would. Bring jokes every time.

14. Offer to do some chauffeuring for a single parent.

15. Start a prayer chain for someone who is ill.

16. Stop arguing. Look at solutions, not problems.

17. Clean up a public space that's been neglected. Plant a tree or flowers, if you can.

18. Volunteer in a classroom, particularly one that is overcrowded or where school aides are in short supply.

19. Take your string or wind instrument outside on a beautiful day and play with your full heart.

20. Love someone unconditionally.

21. When you donate to charity, give new clothes instead of used ones.

22. Help a new neighbor unpack boxes or bring the dinner over. (Don't forget the plates and the tablecloth!)

23. If you're sober, drive a drunken friend home. And if the driver is sober but tired and you're not, take the wheel.

24. Take a leadership role. Be the first to say yes to a needed project. Do so enthusiastically.

There are, of course, hundreds of other ideas that could be added to this list, and I hope you do so. Just one final note about what all of these things have in common: They are what you do because you *can*. The gift of Thanks originates in the idea that you have already received what you need and have something to share with others. A blessing is something that is easy to do and very obvious. An example of this happened to me in a Florida airport. I was traveling home with our daughters (Steve was away on business), and as we stood in line to go through security, I noticed that the man in front of me was having a very agitated conversation with the security guard.

"But I have to go through!" he said in an exasperated voice. "My mother's eighty-four, and she won't know where to go!"

"Listen, no one goes through without a boarding pass," the man said. "And your mother will be just fine. I'm eighty-four, so I know."

When we went through the magnetic arch, they were still arguing. But I did notice that the man never did get to the gate, so obviously the guard held him back.

We sat down to wait for our flight. A few minutes later, a plane arrived, and the passengers disembarked. When they all walked away, one woman was left at the gate. She was elderly and was looking around as if waiting for someone. Knowing what I had just witnessed, I approached her.

"Are you waiting for someone, ma'am?" I asked.

"Oh, yes," she said, "but they're not here."

"Well, they're making everyone wait up in the lobby area," I said. "Could I escort you there?"

She said yes, I took her carry-on bag, and we walked slowly but surely up to the security area. A family was there to greet her—her daughter, son-in-law, and grandchildren. It was not the man's mother, as I had suspected, but nevertheless, this new family was visibly relieved to see their loved one had made it from the gate.

When I returned to my seat, my daughter said, "That was a nice thing to do."

"Yes," I said, "but that wasn't the only reason I did it. I did it because it was mine to do. I heard what the security guard told that man, so when I saw this woman, I knew it was my job. I did it because I could." The family did not need to say thank you. I was thankful that I could help them and their mother.

Blessings are what God can do, and so can we. There is no end to the thankful gifts we can exchange between heaven and Earth.

. . . .

CHAPTER ELEVEN

The Gift of Intention

STEVE AND I married in the early 1970s, fresh from the Age of Aquarius and full of blissful hope. We were very young and wanted to appear very mature at our wedding. So we chose to address each other during ceremony, stating our intentions for our marriage. I went first, and by the time I was done talking about how much I loved him and why I wanted to be his wife, there wasn't a dry eye in the congregation. I intended to commit my life to bringing out the best in him and allowing him to do the same for me. Then it was his turn. He took both my hands in his, looked me straight in the eye, and said, "Robin, when I woke up this morning, I only had one question on my mind." The sanctuary went silent as we all waited to hear the sole object of his wonder.

"WHAT AM I DOING HERE?????"

At that moment, I thought he was going to pull a number from the movie *I Love You, Alice B. Toklas*, turn around and walk out, leaving me at the altar. Steve loved a good joke, but I wasn't sure if I should laugh or scream. Instead, he went on to state his intentions, telling everyone exactly why he was there, because he loved me and intended for our life together to be wonderful.

After everyone in the room had a good laugh and began breathing again, the rabbi spoke. Although he was smiling, he was dead serious.

"Robin and Steve," he said, "the words you just exchanged are very good, because you both intend to make the best life together that you can. But in order for that to happen, I don't wish for you the same happiness you have today. Because from now on, each of you will be changing. And so I wish for you to have the intention, strength, and patience to keep up with each other's changes." Twenty-five years later, I can honestly say that no truer words were ever spoken.

Looking back, I wonder why I was smart enough to declare my intentions that day and why I have been too dumb not to create and share more intentions since. For an intention is a powerful thing. It aligns our deepest hopes and wishes with our thoughts, words, and deeds. It is what lifts us above surviving life to thriving in it. And it's relatively easy to do: Just look at the circumstances you're in, choose how you want to feel, and then grow for it.

Unfortunately, as stated earlier, Dr. Levinson points out in his book that we have no biological mechanism for following through on our intentions. In other words, we're programmed to want the best but built to get something else. And that's why most of us avoid using our gift of Intention. We think we can't have what we want, so we don't bother to make clear decisions. Still, the life force within us continually insists that we try, because we need reasons to discover how good we are and how valuable we can be. When we are at our best, doing what feels right, and appreciating what we've created, we are peaceful. Using our gifts, we have a better-than-average chance of living up to our own highest hopes.

I discovered the gift of Intention months after the flood, when I became restless and unhappy. In spite of our survival and our ability to return to our house, Steve and I found ourselves living in conditions that were out of our control. Talk of a new dike surfaced almost immediately, and when the lines were drawn, the clay wall was set to go right through our living room. Many of our neighbors and others along or near the river in other parts of town were scheduled to suffer the same fate, and dissention began immediately. As the weeks wore on and the uncertainty about the dike placement grew, I found myself losing the peace I had so happily gained.

The city had begun a buyout program of the most heavily damaged houses, and I noticed that many of those who willingly let go of the past—however painful it was for them to do it—seemed to be faring better than those who refused to make change their choice. Although the sellers had no control over what the river had done to their homes, they could decide what would be next for them after the paperwork was done. In other words, their intention was to get on with life, and they seemed to gain energy and forward momentum with it.

That's when I took a good, long walk. What I saw was that the neighborhood I loved was, for the most part, gone. Three of the four houses directly across the street from ours had been condemned as unsafe, and the next four were in the dike line. Neighbors to the east and south were gone for good, as that part of the neighborhood was on lower ground and suffered the worst damage. An enormous orange X was painted on the siding of each of these houses, meaning they were slated to be torn down.

Our own house needed extensive repairs; and we knew that even under the best conditions the construction of the new dike would force us out in a few years. We weren't likely to sink the money or the time into fixing up the house. We had already found evidence of mice in the kitchen and roaches in the basement, both of which had gotten in through the huge cracks we now had in our foundation. It looked like the only sure thing ahead was years of uncertainty and annoyance about what we couldn't do, what wasn't there any longer, and what we didn't want to have happen. To me, that felt like a slow death, and I shuddered at the thought.

By the time I got home, I didn't have a clear decision, but I was absolutely sure of my intention. "I want to be happy," I said to Steve that night. "I don't want to be angry or worried any more. We need to get on with our lives."

Steve nodded in agreement, but he wasn't smiling. "Nobody's going to buy this house right now," he said matter-of-factly. "And in good conscience, we couldn't sell it anyway, knowing that the dike is likely to run right through it."

We talked about moving it, but it was far too high, wide, and long to be maneuvered through the narrow cobblestone streets surrounding it. And even if telephone poles, lights, and trees could somehow be avoided, the house had plaster-and-lathe walls, bricks for insulation, and much of the original, pre-1900s siding and glass. It would likely crumble like a cookie when it was lifted. "I've had enough fixing to last the rest of my life," I said to Steve. "There has to be another alternative."

So every day in my morning meditation, I sat and thought about my intention: feeling happy. I focused on the health and well-being of our family, the faces of the friends we loved, and how I looked and sounded when I was enjoying my life. I didn't ask God for any specific solution, because with circumstances as they were, I couldn't imagine what it would be. My prayers were simply "I intend to feel happy," and for those few minutes every day, I was.

A few weeks later, my intentions met their match. The city offered extend the buyout program to those who were living in their homes but were within the dike line. They offered a generous allowance for relocating within the city, too. It took a few months to negotiate a price, but once we did, we were able to move into a spacious townhome that made us very, very happy. Steve got the photography studio he'd always wanted; I had a home office with a grassy view; the girls got their privacy on the lower level; and we all got an active, thriving neighborhood.

WE ARE NEVER STUCK

The gift of Intention is God's way of guaranteeing that we are never stuck. It answers the questions: *What now? What next?* No matter what mistakes we have made, how grim things may appear to be, or how unhappy we are, we have this tool to help us rise above our circumstances and move forward. This gift does not come with a statute of limitations, so there's no such thing as being too old to use it. It works when we are ill and when we're not. There is nothing too big for it to overcome and nothing too small for it to uplift.

The gift of Intention fills us with the confidence we need to move on with life. It is a cousin to the gift of Faith, except that it puts the power of change directly in our own hands, not God's. That said, it is important to note that intentions that make us feel peaceful often come from our higher self, our "transmission link" to our Creator, that uses our gift of Trust to remind us of whether the choice we've made is a good one for ourselves and all concerned.

The gift of Intention puts us firmly and squarely in the driver's seat of our own lives. Even if we use it to make a wrong turn, it stays with us until we find the way that works best. When we employ it, we feel more capable and become more contented. If we form an intention that is wrong for us or for others, there is always the opportunity to form a new intention that will make things right. That's what happened to John.

JOHN'S STORY

"My partner and I each had twenty years of experience in broadcasting," John says, "And together, we had just made the radio stations where we worked profitable after nine months. So when it became obvious that the stations were going to be sold, we thought we'd try our hand at ownership."

The pair found some investors and purchased the stations. Their intention was to have fun serving the community while continuing to be profitable, but all was not rosy. "Right after we bought the stations, the market changed dramatically," John says. "Deregulation came, and many more stations were added to the market. Radio became a commodity, and the price for advertisements dropped dramatically." He sighed. "We didn't know how to control costs fast enough. Things got worse and worse, and we kept sinking more money into the place. We didn't know how to turn it around."

For three years, John and his partner gave it their best. But the problems didn't subside. "We needed to put in more cash, and I didn't have it," he admits. "Instead, I gave parcels of my stock for my contribution, until eventually they offered to take my name off the note." While that removed the pressure of the stations' growing debt from John's shoulders, he wasn't about to give up on the dream he shared with his friend. The pair split up the management of the operation, with John taking the smaller, as-yet unprofitable AM station and his partner taking the FM. Once again, John intended to make things work.

"We were kind of a David in a Goliath market," he says. "Our station was much smaller and less powerful than our competitors. It got down to assessing myself and my personal strengths, and the market opportunity." John knew he somehow had to be different from everyone else but didn't want to have an all-music format, which was the accepted norm in radio station programming at the time. "I was looking for hope, because I was real down on myself at that point," he admits. "I had those thoughts like 'I wish I had studied more in college.' I was praying for some guidance, just to find a course."

Eventually, it came to him. "In my career, I just happened to work well with agricultural-type accounts because of the farm community in which I was raised, and I also had some previous experience with ag radio," he says. "When I started to analyze the market in our area, it was 95 percent agricultural. The more I looked at it, the more it hit me to create a radio station to serve that market."

And so John took his little AM station and intended to turn it into a farmer's dream come true. "My mission was to superserve farmers and those who wished to do business with them," he said.

John's partner and the other investors were skeptical about the unusual move, until he convinced them through statistics that he was talking about serving a commercially viable market. "They asked if I wasn't putting all my eggs in one basket, so I just showed them the size of the basket," he said with a laugh. "Then I told them that I only needed one employee, the best farm broadcaster in the world."

That man, it turned out, worked for a competitor, and while he was intrigued by John's idea and his passion for it, he was unwilling to give up his security at the number-one station in town. "I asked him how he'd feel about talking farm twenty-five hours in a twenty-four hour day," John explained. "He loved the idea but felt there was no reason to take the job other than sharing the dream." But John wouldn't give up. He asked his partner and the other investors to meet with the broadcaster. "He was impressed with their commitment," John said. "After he talked to them, he said he was willing to do it."

Things started to change very quickly after that. The

broadcaster gave his notice at his old station, but with several weeks until his employment ended, he headed to the National Farm Broadcasters Convention in Kansas City to do live reports. He asked John to accompany him. Once again, trouble reared its head. "When his old employer found out I was there with him, they cleaned out his desk," John said. "So we started to work the convention in earnest, telling everyone we were starting an all-farm radio station. It was 'fish-or-cut-bait' time."

The pair got home and initiated a daily series of farm programming, including market reports every hour. They launched programs that responded to suggestions made by an informal group of fifteen "experts"—farmers and farm wives who would come into town and talk to John while he bought them lunch.

"We'd go out and walk the fields during the growing season," John said. "We went out in a different direction every week and reported on the crop progress." By doing that, the little farm station scored a coup: It was the first to report the appearance of "late blight," the potato disease that caused the potato famine in Ireland. Late blight can wipe out an entire crop in less than a week, so John knew there was no time to waste. "We broke that story on our radio station, and as a result, we learned that a chemical company had sold more than four million dollars' worth of product in one week's time to treat the disease. At that point, I thought, 'Wow! We really *can* effect change.' "

Not much later, John received a call from an advertising agency in San Francisco that bought commercials for twelve times the station's current price. He knew his intentions were moving him in the right direction. "We continued to superserve the farmers," he said with joy. "We'd haul lunch right to the field during harvest and operate their machinery while they ate. We bought $120,000 worth of credit at implement dealerships, turned it into $100 certificates, and discounted the certificates on the air as a contest. We created a promotion with a field service truck that drew crowds everywhere it went."

John and Mike, his farm broadcaster, often worked eighteen-hour days, starting at 3:00 A.M. and going late into the evening. Although they were often tired, their love for what they were doing never lagged, and, eventually, they could see they were making a difference. Farmers began telling John that they were building their own antennaes to pick up his little station. One group signed a petition asking them to get an affiliate to broadcast in their area. And that's when John's intentions really bore fruit.

"We got more and more interested in creating a network," John said. "But the investors didn't want to do the financing. My partner had already left the station, so I could see it was coming to a natural end." Then the phone rang. "The Wheat Growers were interested in getting onto the information highway," he explained. "They asked if we wanted to grow and expand this thing, because they wanted to be a part of it. They basically offered us an open checkbook." He laughed. "I mean to tell you—that was one exciting time of my life.

"So we hired my former partner as a consultant to put the deal together, and he did a marvelous job. We sold them a percentage of the business for cash—just enough for three to four months of operations."

In September 1995, John rented an office for $100, borrowed a desk and dragged a chair up from his basement, and the Red River Farm Network was born. He and his new partners Mike and Jerry bought $5,000 worth of used broadcasting equipment and went to work. "We hoped to sign up six stations and thought utopia would be ten," he said. "But one day, after I'd driven about 450 miles, I came home late and my wife asked, 'So? How was your day?' And I gave her the thumbs up, because we'd just signed station number twelve!" By December 5, just as the initial investment money

THE TEN GIFTS • 189

was running out, the network was broadcasting on its affiliates. Since then, the network has been profitable: "Our business is doubling every year, and our ratings are growing," John said, and John, Mike, Jerry, and the others involved are still having fun.

"In order to feel good, you've got to have felt bad," John said philosophically. "I have a favorite saying: 'May the peace of God disturb you.' My point is that if you don't have it, you should work at it. And when the wind comes up, pray to God *and* row for the shore. I believe you have to combine prayer with action."

As John proved, the gift of Intention can be helpful in getting you back on track when circumstances are at least partially beyond your control or if you are not completely clear about what would make things right. John combined his gift of Intention with his gift of Faith, which surrendered the outcome and opened one door after another.

Sometimes, as in John's case, you're not entirely sure what to do next. Other times, you know *exactly* what you want. Even if circumstances throw you off course, you are unwilling to settle for anything less than what's right for you. In this case, the gift of Intention is best combined with the gift of Character. You know who you are or want to be and intend to get to it. That's what happened to Mary Jean.

MARY JEAN'S STORY

Mary Jean had just finished reading a chapter in her paperback. She set the book on her nightstand, turned off the light, and went into cardiac arrest. She was lucky: Because there was so little traffic late at night, paramedics made it to her house in less than five minutes. "I'm a rare survivor," she admitted. "Ninety-five percent of the people who have this die because they can't get help fast enough."

Mary Jean was unconscious ior two days, and when she

came to, the news wasn't good. "They told my family that if I didn't have an AICD [automatic implantable cardiovascular defibrillator] implanted in my body, I'd have to be hooked up to a machine for the rest of my life." Although she was awake, she could not make the decision for herself. "I was physically able to have the surgery, but my mind wasn't functioning, so I don't remember it," she explained. "I did not recognize people outside my immediate family for a while. I was in the hospital for about a week after the surgery, and I was totally unaware of what was going on."

Mary Jean's family was not surprised: One year earlier, while she was volunteering for the Red Cross in a disaster area, she had been out of breath frequently. After eight days on the job, she ended up in the emergency room, gasping. At that time, the cardiologist did extensive tests and told Mary Jean she needed a heart transplant, except that she was considered too old for it. She had gotten through the year with medication . . . and luck. At the moment, it seemed as if her luck had run out.

But Mary Jean was an active, committed participant in life, and her family knew that being tied to a machine or slowing down just wasn't her style. They had the defibrillator implanted. "I'm a bionic woman," she said with a laugh. "I have wires up into my shoulders and down into my heart."

Getting used to her new situation wasn't easy. "Before this happened, I was the ultimate healthy person. To have something wrong all of a sudden was like 'No! That can't be me, because I'm perfectly healthy.' " She let that thought guide her intentions. "At first, I was thinking that I couldn't do what I wanted to do and had always been doing. But then I knew I had a choice: I could go into despair and decide I was going to die, or I could go on. I've known several people who've had this surgery and do nothing, because they're convinced they're going to die. But I wake up every day and say 'Wow! I'm here!' I keep going because that's my nature. I'm a survivor. It's my heritage. And my family has been extremely supportive."

Fortunately, the first thing restored was her memory. When she left the hospital, it was a beautiful day. "I stepped back on my heels because of the brightness of the sun, and I said, 'Where am I? What are we doing here?' I just clicked out of it, and I was okay after that. My total memory was restored." In all, she lost two weeks of memory, "but I was fortunate because some people lose months, or even years."

But she was dogged by the inconvenience of illness. "I was told I couldn't drive," she said, "and that was the worst thing, especially after raising six children and having some freedom. I was also advised that I should never swim alone, because if the machine went off, I could lose consciousness. And I love to swim."

But Mary Jean intended to live a normal life and went back to the activities she enjoyed. The newly implanted machine, however, seemed to have other plans for her. "I had five zaps the first year after I had this installed," she said. "One time I became so excited after performing with the Green Valley Chorus, I started to feel a little lightheaded and flushed. That's the sign that this [heart arrhythmia] could be happening. I was also active in the Senior Olympics. At a swim meet, I was excited and rushing toward my lane, and I got zapped." She made it over to the lane divider and slowly walked out of the pool that day, but sometimes, she admitted, she isn't so lucky. "It can be very serious; I can pass out."

In spite of her concerns, Mary Jean pressed on, staying true to her intention to be herself. "When I make up my mind to do something, I do it," she explained. "I was determined to try everything again." The first thing she did was take care of the house by herself. After that, she encouraged her husband to go back to his thrice-weekly golf game. While he was gone, she walked the neighborhood.

"The hospital has get-togethers, and the people who've had this surgery talk about how to live. I listen to what some of the others are doing, and I hear them say you can get off your duff and do anything you feel like doing. But so many people won't go shopping or do anything alone. And I think, 'Their spouses must be basket cases!' "

Now, five years after her first cardiac arrest, things are mostly back to normal. At the time of this writing, Mary Jean is finishing a three-year term as one of six national directors of Sigma Alpha Iota, an international music fraternity for women. She's active with the Tucson Opera League and is Neighborhood Watch chairperson for her subdivision. She swims laps with her husband at the pool in her neighborhood and volunteers two hours every week as a pool monitor. She's also the social chair of her subdivision. Best of all, because she hasn't had an episode in over three years, she's been cleared to drive again.

In a program that Mary Jean presented at the Alpha Gamma Delta IRD day, she expressed her philosophy on life after "death." "Do something today that you've never done before. Think 'tomorrow.' Make an appointment today for six months from now. Even though you feel you may not live very long, you still have the intent to do so, and live for it."

There are some concessions she makes to her condition, however. She has to have her defibrillator monitored every three months, and recently she had surgery to implant a new one that will last five to seven years. Having a machine the size of a deck of cards under the skin near her waist means that she has to wear blousy tops, but she says that most people don't notice.

She and her husband also travel. "I'm part gypsy," she said with a laugh. "We take a cruise every year, and we're leaving for Alaska soon."

Mary Jean lives life to the fullest every day. "I've learned one important lesson," she said. "You've got to enjoy things.

If you're not, then don't do it. I'm much more able to say no now, because I only do what I want to do.

"I'm optimistic about my life now," she added. "We're celebrating our fiftieth wedding anniversary this year, and I never dreamed we'd make it. My philosophy now is either 'Just do it,' or 'You can, you can, you *can*.' "

With the gift of Intention, we can indeed do or be or have anything we have in our minds and hearts. When you use this gift, you will automatically find yourself using your other nine gifts, because it delivers you to life fully and completely. And once you are here, you will see that there is more good than bad, more safety than danger, more help than hurt.

As we are fond of saying in the Jewish tradition, *"L'chaim!"* (To life!)

PEACE PROGRESS STEP 11

. . . .

"I Feel Good!"

The gift of Intention isn't meant to be used once in a lifetime, such as only at your wedding. Because intention is foresight, not hindsight, it's best used to decide how you want to feel *in advance* of your actions. The reason so many of us get in trouble in our lives is because we never set our intentions; we simply plow into life headfirst, and take whatever we get.

The gift of Intention is the easiest and most pleasant of the ten to use. If you don't have a specific goal in mind, choose a feeling you want to have. Then simply close your eyes, think, and say, "I intend to feel peaceful." (Or happy, safe, free, connected, etc. Choose a feeling state of mind that you believe will work to better the situation you're in.) Keep your eyes closed and stay quiet for a moment until you feel a shift in your demeanor. Then open your eyes and go about your day.

Doing this sounds a little like making a wish, but there's a difference. The gift of Intention is not like a genie in a bottle, where you get one desire fulfilled and that's it. Instead, you will find it works best when you use it to form the same intentional feeling several times *every day*. For example, say you state your intention to feel peaceful that day, and the first thing that hits you when you get to the office is a huge project you weren't prepared to tackle. Before you do anything, stop and think, "I intend to feel peaceful," and then look at the pile, memo, or phone message. I guarantee that you will see things differently: Instead of feeling shattered and lost, you will become clearer about who might help you (gift of Unity), what might make this fun (gift of Courage), or see a silver lining that might answer a bigger, deeper yearning (gift of Dreams). If a colleague rushes over, interrupting whatever you've started to ask you a question, you can remind yourself "I intend to feel peaceful" before you answer him or her. And at the end of the day, if you're leaving a mountain of work behind, you can say "I intend to feel peaceful" as you're putting the key in the lock of your door at home and discover that your worries won't be able to accompany you into the house. As you do this repeatedly, you will notice that disturbances don't bother you as much, and you will, indeed, feel peaceful. You will also begin to attract circumstances that are more in line with your intentions, so ambushes such as the one just described don't happen as often.

If your life is going pretty well, all things considered, and you're not looking for a major shift, use your gift of Intention just to smooth over the rough edges. If the phone rings while you're in the middle of doing something, think "I intend for this interruption to be short" and watch how your thoughts and words follow your intention. If you're grabbing a fast food meal on the run, you can think "I intend to enjoy this food," and the flavors will pop in your mouth while the guilt disappears. If you run into an old friend, you can think "I intend for this to be pleasant," and undoubtedly you will come away with a kind memory of the conversation.

If you're like Mary Jean and know what you want, state that in your intention: "I intend to be healthy and independent." Again, remind yourself of your intention continuously, even if circumstances suggest otherwise at the moment. Eventually, your experience will shift in the way you want.

The gift of Intention is a way we can program our subconscious to focus on what we want. While the gift of Faith implies "What *don't* I want?" the gift of Intention wants to know "What *do* I want?" After you decide, you only have to believe that, with practice, you will always get what you intend.

By now, I hope that using your other gifts has proven to you, that life is safer and more fun than you once believed. Use your tenth gift, and you will be delivered to life in new and pleasant ways. Then you'll know that peace is within your grasp.

. . . .

A New Life

IT IS CHALLENGING to drive around Grand Forks and East Grand Forks these days. More than two years after the flood, our roads are still being repaired, our sewers replaced. The central bridge connecting our two towns was closed for over a month while an invisible wall dike was added on the east side. Both downtowns are a labyrinth of orange detour signs and fences.

But if you look up and around instead of down or even straight ahead, you can see the future clearly. Both towns have beautiful new elementary and middle school campuses that are open and functioning. New neighborhoods have been built, and families are moving into them. Our churches have been repaired, expanded, or built anew. A new civic center, the Aurora, is under construction.

In a few more years, our twin towns will likely have more new infrastructure than any other established metro area in America. Our arts and entertainment industries will be thriving, and our governmental agencies, newly clustered in a single downtown area, will be more accessible than ever. Business will have settled into some kind of predictable pattern. We will have our pride in all of this, as will the tens of thousands of people around the country who helped make it happen.

For those of us who lived through the flood, we will have relief. The worst will be over, including most of the process of recovery. We will have the confidence that we can survive a life-shattering event. But we also will have something else: an unspoken fear that sometime, somehow, it could happen again.

Those of you who have ever suffered a dark night of the soul know what I mean. You get through it, you get past it, and you go on . . . or not. Even though you are stronger and wiser, you cringe when certain dates come up on the calendar.

USING YOUR GIFTS ELIMINATES FEAR

I once read that love and fear cannot exist simultaneously, so as long as we harbor dread, we shut out the promise of what our lives could be. That's why the gifts are so important. Day by day, they show us clear alternatives to what frightens us or holds us back. The gifts live deep inside us, in the same place where fear tends to hide: in our gut. Up to now, if you haven't realized that, it's only because you were paying attention to the squeaky wheel, not the one that is running smoothly, silently.

God has given us life and everything we need to sustain and enjoy it. But when we allow our fears to call the shots, no job, house, vacation, income, relationship, body tone or cholesterol reading will ever satisfy our souls. Worse, the dark side casts shadows on every other human being, so that we see others not as collaborators in our happiness but as competitors. Fear makes us think that life is a game we can't win.

But with the gifts, everything looks different. Each event and situation becomes a means to use our gifts, and with them, we can take something as big as trouble, shaping and creating out of it something better than before. We can see the limits circumstances place upon us as walls waiting for doors. The gifts become the door frame; it's up to us to add the hinges, wood, and knobs.

Making lifetime use of our gifts requires a change in thinking. Instead of feeling that we must suffer silently, we can demonstrate joy. We no longer have to face down our worst fears; we can play our way around them. We can stop looking askance at every other person and choose instead to see the horizon in their eyes. With the gifts, we can do it. It just takes some practice.

How Long Does It Take?

Change is difficult, not simply because it is a journey into the unknown but because we grow restless and unsure of ourselves too easily. We moan like children: "Why aren't we there yet?"

When Moses was trying to lead the Israelites to the Promised Land, they spent most of their time complaining. In their minds, there was a constant separation between where they were and where they wanted to be. One wonders how different biblical history might be if they had spent those same forty years using their newfound freedom to exercise their gifts. Had they done so, they might have realized that they had already been delivered to life; now all they had to do was live it, regardless of their geography.

Instead, they kept making preparations for what, ironically, most of them would never experience. We do that, too. You may be thinking "After I feel better, then I'll use my gifts," or "I'll look for my gifts the next time I'm in trouble." You can choose to think of your gifts only as emergency first aid, but if you do, you're missing the point. If you recognize them as the constant companions they are, they can not only restore your peace after it has been broken; they can provide support so that your life never falls apart again.

You don't need to wait for things to get better to use your gifts. Start today.

DON'T MISS THE FUN!

If you don't use your gifts every day, you're missing out on a lot of fun. It's great sport to walk into a meeting where there's a problem in the table and be able to sit back confidently while everyone else fumes about it. When the headaches and frustrations have made a huge mess of things, you can pull out your gift of Courage and pipe in with "Well, we know what won't work and what is going to be an uphill climb. And we know we don't want to do, either. What would be fun to try instead?"

Who can resist the opportunity to lift a fallen child, calling on your gift of Love to see the best in him when he sees the worst in himself? Why would you want to miss out on the delicious surprises of surrendering an opportunity to God with your gift of Faith?

It's all yours right now, and you don't have to earn it, suffer for it, or wait for it. Amazing, isn't it?

With the gifts, you can surrender any problem, see love in every person you meet, design your own happiness, and have fun making it come to life. You'll have hands and hearts to help you, and feel a deep sense of satisfaction as things fall into place. You'll be able to trust yourself and other people, and decide the role you want to play on life's stage. As you do, you'll find that you are an agent of blessing, a valuable contributor to the well-being of others. And if, for some unforeseen reason, you go off course, you now have a way to get right back on track. The only thing you have to do is make the choice to use what is already yours.

THE GIFTS HELP YOU MOVE THROUGH CHANGE PEACEFULLY

The world is changing rapidly, and it has little to do with the new millennium. Thanks to stunning advances in communications technology, we are now more aware than ever of what we don't want and what isn't working in the world. The life force within us demands, more than ever, that something must be done. We want things to be better, and we want the improvement to come as quickly as possible. Like it or not, things are changing and will continue to change.

By using your gifts, that change will come more peacefully not just for you but for whatever corner of the world you inhabit. If you are downsized out of a job, you can grab your gift of Dreams and start creating a new job you'd like even better. If you make friends on the Internet with someone who lives on the other side of the planet, you can use your gift of Unity to create a way for you to meet. If the famine in Third World countries disturbs you, you can use your Gift of Intention to find a way you can help eliminate it.

Not everyone has global hopes, and the gifts are perfect for making changes in your individual private life. Use Love to deepen a relationship; Character to grow your own personality; Thanks for paving the way for a coworker or friend to be more peaceful.

When you use your gifts to create or ride the tides of change, you will never be lost. And that feels good. Peaceful.

THE GIFTS IN ACTION

As stated earlier, I think of the gifts as spiritual verbs. Although the names are nouns, they suggest particular actions that lead to enhanced personal peace. If you perform these actions, you see that each gift is a marker on the road to a more satisfied life. Together they tell us exactly what we need to do to improve our sense of calm and contentment:

Faith = Surrender   Joy = Share
Love = Look   Trust = Listen
Dreams = Allow   Character = Choose
Courage = Play   Thanks = Bless
Unity = Ask   Intention = Believe

It is easy to remember and use the gifts this way. To show you how it works, let's use the fictional example of "Joe."

Joe's business was in trouble. After years of declining sales and rising expenses, he had maxed out his debt load and found himself struggling to survive. But he knew, deep down, that he wanted to be a successful entrepreneur. Knowing that answering to his fears hadn't gotten him what he wanted, he decided to use his gifts, instead.

The first thing he did was *surrender* the debts to God. He knew he was in over his head and would need some heavenly help to get restarted. "Take 'em, Lord!" was what he prayed, and immediately, he felt the burden lift. The debts did not disappear magically, but at that instant, Joe realized the importance of not managing his debt but getting rid of it as soon as possible.

That felt good to him, so he went to his telemarketing team and *looked*. Although everything they said and did wasn't exactly as Joe would do it, he could see that they were doing many, many things correctly, creatively, and with confidence. Joe complimented some of them on what he saw and walked away smiling.

As he did, his Gift of Dreams called for his attention. He *allowed* himself to enjoy the pleasant thought of his business thriving, with his bank of telephones ringing day and night. His computer screens were lit, orders were being taken, and boxes were being filled in his warehouse. He could see a stream of red, white, and blue trucks arriving at his shipping door and a mail carrier coming in the front office with a sack filled with letters from satisfied customers. He looked down and saw that his black shoes had the freshly polished gleam of a successful business owner. His new car was parked out front of the building—a silver sedan with a sunroof and a stereo with eight speakers. On his desk was a picture of his wife and sons smiling on their ski vacation. Next to it was a loan statement from his bank marked "Paid in Full" in rich, black ink.

The next day, Joe went to the office with a new hat. It had six multicolored feathers glued to it—one for each member of his telemarketing team. "I think of each of you as a feather in my cap," he said, "someone I'm proud to have working with me. Each customer you satisfy is another feather in my cap, too. So watch this!" At that moment, the phone rang, and one of his associates took good care of the customer. Joe took a feather from the sack he had brought, dabbed it with glue, and added it to the hat. "See?" he said *playfully*, "from now on, each time one of you does a great job like that, I'll add another feather. I bet it won't be long before you have me looking like a chicken!"

Joe's hat was a big hit, companywide. He added one feather for each employee and then *asked* if they would like to get in on the game. The answer was a resounding "Yes!" of course, and so the supervisors joined in, gluing on additional feathers every time one of them "caught" an employee doing something right.

As the months went on, sales surged. Joe took every extra dollar to pay down on his debt. By the end of the year, the company was showing a profit. Joe *shared* his joy by showing up at the company Christmas party wearing what had now become a fully feathered suit, which delighted not only his employees but their spouses and children, as well.

Three years later, the debt was almost gone and sales were still growing in double digits. Joe's phone rang, this time with a call from a lawyer suggesting that Joe go public in an IPO. "You'll be richer than you ever dreamed," he promised.

Joe thought back to his dream. While his family had been living more prosperously, they were still very careful with money. If he went public, he would be able to afford not only a luxury car and the ski vacations but much, much more.

Joe closed his eyes and tried to imagine what his life would be like heading up a company that was traded publicly. At first, all he could see was that he was very, very rich. That should have made him happy, but something was bothering him. He *listened* to a small voice inside him that said "If you go public, you'll have to answer to your stockholders." And a board of directors, he thought, and probably, one or more banks. As someone who was just finishing paying off a huge debt, he realized that he didn't want to start the cycle all over again, no matter how good the reason.

Joe listened to his heart, and made a difficult *choice*. "I'm happiest as a successful entrepreneur, not as the elected CEO of a publicly held company," he said to the lawyer. "Thanks anyway." When he hung up the phone, he felt as light and free as he did when he first imagined what his business could be. "I'll earn what I want," Joe said out loud. "And I'll still have time to be a great father, husband, and friend."

As the years passed, Joe's business continued to thrive. His debts disappeared, and he had plenty of cash in his pocket. It was usual for him to slip some into an envelope and leave it anonymously in the handbag of an employee or the mail slot of a neighbor who was struggling with extra bills. "I've been there," he said to his wife. "I know what a *blessing* a few extra dollars can be sometimes."

Joe lived his life as he intended: happy, healthy, successful, and free. When diabetes struck him later in life, he felt sorry for himself only for a little while. He *believed* he could improve and decided to use it as an opportunity to alter his diet and learn more about taking better care of himself. "After all, I don't want to miss a minute," he said to his wife.

Joe used his gifts, and his life became a gift to the world around him. You can, too.

LIVE YOUR GIFTS, GET YOUR PEACE

If you opened this book restless and unhappy, my prayers are that you leave it in a far more peaceful frame of mind and being. If you were drawn here to expand on your already-established peace, I trust you have a refreshed radiance that will encourage you to go out and share your light with the world. Ralph Waldo Emerson was right: No one can give you peace but yourself. Now that you know about your gifts, there is only one thing left to do: Live them.

As for me, I have learned that there is no better time than right now to start feeling better. While I love the life I have been able to create using my gifts since the flood, it is not perfect, and I am not a walking example of bliss. Because of them, however, I have complete confidence that my future is within my control, regardless of what the weather, other people, or the river may do. The gifts have taught me how to truly cherish those who populate my life and have given me new reasons to enjoy their triumphs. Using my gifts, I find it better to say yes only to those things that I can commit to with my full heart, and I no longer feel guilty when I have to say no. I use my gifts daily, which helps keep me calm when others are upset, centered when things go wrong, and enthusiastic for what I do and who I'm with.

Although I am learning how to use my gifts, there is one thing about them of which I am absolutely, positively certain: Using them has made me more peaceful. Although I am actually busier now than I was just a few years ago (ironically, when I thought I was stressed to the max!), I no longer spew fire when someone asks me to do something or get defensive when I am criticized. Because I know that everyone has these gifts, I am more patient with others. I look for the good in them, and I am consistently rewarded for the effort.

But further, knowing I have the gifts has enabled me to take risks I never would have otherwise. Using my gift of Courage, I launched an online course entitled "Ignore Your Problems and They'll Go Away," and delighted in helping people nationwide get rid of some of the things that were holding them back from their happiness. With my gift of Intention, I started investing in stocks to help stabilize our financial future and am now reading books and talking about financial planning. My gift of Joy is coming in handy these days, too, as I spend more time writing notes to friends and family to tell them to share news and send love.

Peace for You, and Everyone Else

In the last lines of the Passover seder service, we say in unison, "Peace! Peace to us, and to everyone!" I used to think that was a call to put an end to war on Earth, but now I believe it is more than that. We must find peace in our own hearts before we can either find or create it anywhere else. We have been in exile from ourselves, searching everywhere but in our own hearts for what we want and need. It is time to come home, the place where true and lasting personal peace resides.

Using our gifts, we can stop running from life and, instead, deliver ourselves to it with unfettered hearts. When we do, we will stop feeling as if there isn't enough, that time is running out, that love is lost, and that trust is broken.

Instead, we will experience, perhaps for the first time in our lives, that there is enough of everything for everyone.

I wish you great joy in discovering your gifts. But above all, I wish you peace.

. . . .

A Prayer for Peace

Creator, Friend, Lover of Life—
I bring You my peace.
It is the best that it can be right now,
And I offer it with all my heart and soul.
Deliver me to those who are ready to share it,
Willing to be a blessing to one another, and to You.
Help me to use my gifts fearlessly,
So that my presence brings joy to the life of the world.
Be with me, God, in every moment
As the love and beauty that inspires good.
Fill me with yes,
Yes . . .
Ten thousand times: "Yes!"
For I am here to embrace the life You have given me.
Let there be peace for me and for everyone
Today, and always.
Amen.

For Further Information

It is always uplifting to make contact with those who are actively using their gifts. To that end, you might want to learn more about some of the organizations and people who are featured in this book. Here is how you can contact them:

Gift of Faith:
Kathy or Randy
c/o Josiah's Hope Foundation
843 Bluff St.
Beloit, WI 53511

Gift of Courage:
Patrick of Pennington
c/o Thief River Linens
230 LaBree Ave. South
Thief River Falls, MN 56701

Gift of Courage:
Dakota Science Center
4275 University Ave.
Grand Forks, ND 58203

Gift of Unity/Vera McKenna:
Close Calls (title of book)*
P.O. Box 144
Crookston, MN 56716-0144

*If ordering, enclose check for $12, made out to "Book Fund."

Gift of Joy:
John D. Odegard
School of Aerospace Sciences
University of North Dakota
Grand Forks, ND 58202

Gift of Intention:
Red River Farm Network
212 South 4th St.
Suite 605
Grand Forks, ND 58201